CULTURE SMART!

BHUTAN

THE ESSENTIAL GUIDE TO CUSTOMS & CULTURE

KARMA CHODEN AND DORJI WANGCHUK

KUPERARD

"The real voyage of discovery consists not in seeking new landscapes, but in having new eyes."

Adapted from Marcel Proust, *Remembrance of Things Past*.

ISBN 978 1 78702 252 2

British Library Cataloguing in Publication Data
A CIP catalogue entry for this book is available
from the British Library

First published in Great Britain
by Kuperard, an imprint of Bravo Ltd
59 Hutton Grove, London N12 8DS
Tel: +44 (0) 20 8446 2440
www.culturesmart.co.uk
Inquiries: publicity@kuperard.co.uk

Design Bobby Birchall
Printed in Turkey by Elma Basım

ABOUT THE AUTHOR

KARMA CHODEN is the founder of Simply Bhutan Travels and a freelance writer. She has a degree in English Literature from the University of North Bengal, India, worked as a journalist for many years with *Kuensel*, Bhutan's national newspaper, and served as a commissioner and focal person for the National Commission for Women and Children in Bhutan.

DORJI WANGCHUK is a management consultant working in London. He has a degree in engineering from the National Institute of Technology in Calicut, India, and an MBA from the University of Cambridge. He was a civil servant in the Bhutanese government for many years, and gives regular talks on developments in Bhutan.

COVID-19
The coronavirus pandemic of 2020 affected millions of people around the world, causing unprecedented social and economic disruption. As the impact of this global crisis continues to unfold, in many countries social norms are being challenged, and enduring changes will be reflected in future editions of Culture Smart! titles.

CONTENTS

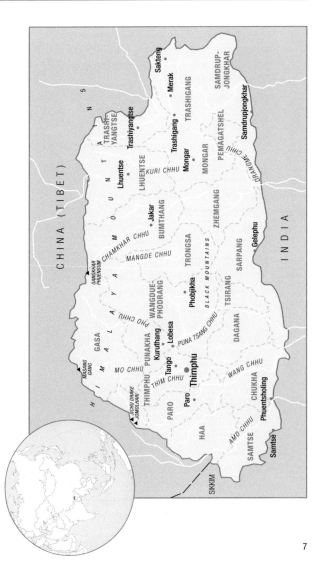

Until recently many people had never heard of
Bhutan, and many of those who had knew little about
it, probably thinking of it as a mystical, faraway land
hidden in the folds of the Himalayas—or "the last
Shangri-la," as it was often referred to by those
adventurous few who made it to its valleys.

Today, however, Bhutan is known all over the
world for three things: for its pursuit of happiness
as the goal of development; for Buddhism as its
predominant way of life; and for its unspoiled
natural environment. With more than 70 percent
of the country under forest cover, and thanks to its
continuous conservation efforts, Bhutan has emerged
as the only carbon-negative country in the world.

The Bhutanese people consider themselves
blessed both by great Buddhist masters and by the
benevolence of the kings of the Wangchuck dynasty;
as being rich in traditional culture and customs; and
as having a sense of purpose in a world driven by
globalization and material pursuits. Gross National
Happiness (GNH)—Bhutan's unique philosophy
of development that focuses on more than just
conventional economic growth by giving equal
priority to environmental conservation and cultural
preservation—challenges the world to reconsider
its ideas about progress and wellbeing.

As Bhutan has gradually emerged from its self-
imposed isolation over the last fifty-plus years, it
has been careful with its choices, and the process of
modernization and development has been deliberately
slow. Roads, hospitals, and schools have been built,

but television and the Internet did not arrive until 1999. English has been embraced as the medium of instruction in schools, but children wear national dress as their school uniform.

Bhutan has opened its doors to the world, but has restricted the inflow of visitors with a "high-value, low-impact" tourism policy, ensuring steady foreign exchange earnings while protecting its unique society from undue outside influence.

In 2008 Bhutan made a giant leap and became the world's youngest democracy, giving way from absolute to constitutional monarchy—a historic change that came not through popular demand but directly from the throne, initiated by the fourth king, His Majesty Jigme Singye Wangchuck. Bhutan faces the issues of any emerging third-world country, such as rising debt and youth unemployment, but it is well positioned through its education and economic policies to manage the economy without significant distress.

Culture Smart! Bhutan aims to give the reader an insight into the country's history, values, customs, and age-old traditions. It describes the historical circumstances that have shaped the Bhutanese people and their way of life. It debunks some myths and helps you to discover this fascinating country for yourself. It highlights changes in attitudes and behavior as the country modernizes, while offering guidance on how to develop a rapport with the Bhutanese and forge meaningful friendships.

Official Name	Kingdom of Bhutan	Locally known as Drukyul (Land of the Thunder Dragon)
Capital City	Thimphu	Pop. of Thimphu city (est. 115,000)
Major Towns	Phuentsholing, Gelephu, Paro, Mongar, Samdrupjongkhar	
Area	14,826 square miles (38,400 sq. km)	
Climate	Alpine, temperate, and subtropical	
Currency	Bhutanese ngultrum (Nu.) (100 chetrum)	Pegged to and on a par with the Indian rupee.
Population	772,000	
Life Expectancy	71.8 for women; 71.1 for men	
GDP Per Capita	US $3,423	
Literacy Rate	71.4%	
Government	Constitutional monarchy. The king is the head of state and the elected prime minster the executive head of the government.	Bicameral legislature: National Council (Upper House) and National Assembly (Lower House). Parliamentary elections are held every five years.
Administrative Divisions	There are 20 districts (*dzongkhag*): Bumthang, Chukha, Dagana, Gasa, Haa, Lhuentse, Mongar, Paro, Permagatshel, Punakha, Samdrupjongkhar, Samtse, Sarpang, Thimphu, Trashigang, Trashiyangtse, Trongsa, Tsirang, Wangduephodrang, Zhemgang	

Ethnic Makeup	Broadly, Drukpa (Ngalong and Sharchokpa) and Lhotshampa (Nepali immigrant descendants)	
Language	Official: Dzongkha	Other languages and dialects include Sharchopkha or Tshangla, Bumthangkha, Kurtopkha, Khyengkha, Chocha Ngacha, and Nepali.
Religion	The main religion is Mahayana Buddhism (Tantric form).	Main Buddhist sects: Drukpa Kaygu and Nyingmapa (75%); Hindus over 20%
Media	*Druk Neytshuel*, *Druk Yoedzer*, and *Gyalchi Sarshog* are Dzongkha-language weekly papers. *Kuensel* is daily and prints in both Dzongkha and English. *Bhutan Times*, *The Journalist*, *The Bhutanese*, *Bhutan Today*, and *Business Bhutan* are English weeklies.	Bhutan Broadcasting Services (BBS) TV and BBS Radio have nationwide coverage. Kuzu FM, Radio Valley 99.9 FM, Yiga Radio 94.7 FM, and Centennial Radio 101 FM cover Thimphu only.
TV/Video	PAL system	
Internet Domain	.bt	
Telephone	Bhutan's country code is 00975.	
Time	GMT + 6 hours	EST + 11 hours

CHAPTER ONE

LAND *&* PEOPLE

GEOGRAPHICAL SNAPSHOT

Bhutan is a landlocked country lying between 89°
and 92° east and 27° and 28° north. Its immediate
neighbors are India, which surrounds it in the west
(Sikkim), south (West Bengal and Assam), and east
(Arunachal Pradesh); and China, with which it shares
its entire northern border. It was an important part of
the trade route to Tibet, particularly to Tibet's Chumbi
Valley, connecting India with Lhasa, Tibet's capital.

Bhutan is about 186 miles (300 km) long and
about 93 miles (150 km) wide, encompassing an
area of around 14,826 square miles (38,400 sq. km),
roughly the size of Switzerland, with elevations
ranging from 984 feet (300 m) in the southern
foothills to 22,965 feet (7,000 m) in the north.
Great geographical and climatic variations provide a
perfect setting for a rich and spectacular biodiversity.

TERRAIN

Bhutan is a mountainous land, which consists of three broad physiographical zones: the southern belt, made up of the Himalayan foothills adjacent to the flatlands along the Indian border; the inner Himalayas, consisting of the main river valleys and steep mountains; and the high Himalayas, featuring alpine meadows and snow-capped mountains.

The southern foothills, also called the Terai region, run from 984 feet (300 m) to 3,281 feet (1000 m) in elevation. Except for a narrow strip of flatland and some terrace farming, most of the foothills are densely forested. This area, extending across the border to India, is called The Duars (Sanskrit for "passes"), with each *duar* named after a river that runs through it. These lands were once under the control of the Bhutanese before they were annexed by British

India following wars leading up to the 1865 Treaty of Sinchula.

The mid-region, the inner Himalayas, is mostly comprised of valleys and forested hillsides ranging from 3,609 feet (about 1,100 m) to 11,483 feet (about 3,500 m) in elevation, and occupies the largest part of the country. Most of the major towns in Bhutan, including the capital city, Thimphu, lie in this belt. The topography features broad valleys, deep gorges, and fast-flowing rivers. Only a few valleys are suitable for extensive farming, with most of the hillsides still covered in forests. Most of the high passes between towns, such as the Dochhu-la (10,006 ft; 3,050 m), Pelela (11,483 ft; 3,500 m), Yotongla (11,237 ft; 3,425 m), and Thrumshingla (12,402 ft; 3,780 m) lie within this band, often becoming secondary watersheds for major rivers such as the Manas in Assam, India.

The northern part of the country, separated from Tibet by a chain of glacial mountains with several peaks over 22,500 feet (7,000 m), is a part of the Greater Himalayas. It remains snowbound throughout the year, and forms a watershed with waters that flow south into India's great Brahmaputra River. While most rivers flow south, there are a few that flow into Tibet from the northern mountains. This part of the country remains inaccessible for most of the year. Some of the highest peaks, traversing from west to east, include Jomolhari (23,996 ft; 7,314 m), Jichu Drake (22,881 ft; 6,974 m), Masang Gang (23,484 ft; 7,158 m), Tsherigang (23,163 ft; 7,060 m), Gangkar Phuensum (24,738 ft; 7,540 m), and Kuhla Gangri (24,783 ft; 7,554 m). Bhutan as a Buddhist country reveres nature, and a number of these mountains remain unclimbed and unexplored as they are regarded as the abodes of gods and deities and not to be soiled by human activity. Gangkar Phuensum remains the highest unclimbed peak in the world.

CLIMATE

Bhutan experiences great variations in climate, given its topography and variant altitudes. The southern foothills enjoy a subtropical climate with a monsoon season: hot, humid summers, when temperatures reach 97°F (36°C) from April to June, followed by a monsoon rain respite; and warm, balmy winters, with temperatures of 59°F (15°C). The southern belt receives a significant amount of rainfall, as high as 197 inches (5,000 mm) a year. The heavy rain often causes travel havoc, with landslides completely washing away parts of roads and destroying bridges, stranding travelers for days. The far north, above 14,763 feet (4,500 m) has a harsh climate, with most areas permanently covered in snow and ice. The lower-lying northern areas enjoy a few months free of ice and snow in the summer, usually between June and August, during which most of the trekking expeditions popular with tourists are undertaken.

In the mid-belt temperate region, where the major towns are located and most of the tourist activities are concentrated, summers can be hot, with temperatures up to 86°F (30°C) from May until mid-July, before the onset of the monsoon, which lasts until September. The winter months from November until mid-February are dry, with temperatures averaging 59°F (15°C) to 65°F (18°C) during the days, and plenty of sunshine and clear blue skies. By contrast, the temperatures drop below the freezing point at night. There is snow in some valleys, such as Thimphu, Bumthang, Paro, and Haa, during the winter, but it does not last long on the valley floors; the surrounding mountains remain covered in snow.

The best times to visit the country are in spring and fall. Spring arrives in February and lasts until mid-May, when the whole countryside is a lush green and comes alive with wild flowers in full bloom— particularly rhododendrons, locally called *etho metho*, of which there are forty-six different species in the wild jungles of Bhutan. Every April there is a three-day Rhododendron Festival at Lamperi Botanical Park, near Thimphu, to celebrate the flowers in their natural habitat.

September sees the last of the big rains as the monsoon retreats to usher in the pleasant season of fall, with blue skies and sunny days. Although it can be chilly at night the days are warm, and this is the perfect season to trek and explore the wilderness.

FLORA AND FAUNA

Bhutan is blessed with an outstanding natural environment, and is recognized as a global biodiversity hotspot. Within the three broad physiographical zones, Bhutan has recorded the existence of 5,603

A spotted tiger lily, one of Bhutan's many native plants.

species of vascular plants, including 369 species of orchid and the 46 species of rhododendron mentioned above. Of the recorded plant species, 105 species are found nowhere else in the world.

Mammal species in the wild number close to two hundred, and Bhutan is home to some of the world's most threatened species, such as the Bengal tiger, snow leopard, Asian elephant, red panda, golden langur, and takin—Bhutan's national animal. Bird life is also impressive: 678 species have been recorded, including 14 globally threatened species, which include the rare black-necked cranes that come to roost every winter in the central and eastern valleys.

Bhutan has demonstrated a strong will and leadership in maintaining this rich natural biodiversity: Over 42 percent of the country has been declared as protected

areas, which include five national parks, four wildlife
sanctuaries, and a strict nature reserve.

These protected areas are connected by biological
corridors, amounting to 8.61 percent of the country, to
ensure the contiguity of the natural habitats and allow
the movement of wildlife between them. Having
started such development in recent years, Bhutan has
been able to learn from the mistakes of others.

Forests account for more than 70 percent of the
country's land cover—one of the highest in the
world, with the constitution mandating that at least
60 percent of Bhutan is maintained under forest cover
at all times. As a result of this vast forest cover and the
limited number of polluting industries, Bhutan is
among the few countries in the world with net negative
greenhouse gas emissions.

The takin, Bhutan's national animal.

PEOPLE

While Bhutan covers an area similar to Switzerland's, its population is minuscule in comparison. The current estimated population is 772,000—the lowest population density of all countries in South Asia. Bhutan's population growth has stabilized over the last decade, growing at a rate of around 2 percent. However, the pressure is on urban areas, where rural migrants increasingly come to seek opportunities.

The population is mostly concentrated along the east–west lateral highway in the central valleys and along the southern belt of the country. It is often broadly broken down into two groups—the Drukpa (people of the north, of Tibetan and indigenous–Burmese origin) and the Lhotshampa (people of the south, of Nepalese origin). The Drukpa are further divided into Ngalong, people from western Bhutan, and Sharchokpa, literally "people from the east."

The Ngalong (or Ngalop) inhabit the valleys of western Bhutan stretching from Haa to Wangduephodrang. They are believed to have descended from Tibetan immigrants as far back as the ninth century, similar to the semi-nomadic inhabitants of the northwestern regions of Lingzhi, Laya, Gasa, and the Lunana highlands. They speak Dzongkha, the official national language.

The Sharchokpa of eastern Bhutan, the most populous group, are believed to be of indigenous–Burmese descent and speak Tshangla, a Tibeto–Burman language. The Ngalong and Sharchokpa together comprise around 75 percent of the overall population and are predominantly Buddhist.

Ngalong men in national dress.

The Lhotshampa dominate the southern foothills, and are fourth- and fifth-generation descendants of Nepali immigrants who settled in the late nineteenth and early twentieth centuries. They represent numerous Nepali-speaking ethnic groups such as the Chhetri, Gurung, Rai, Limbu, and Newar, and form around 25 percent of the population. They have maintained their distinct culture, their traditional dress, and their Nepali language, and are mainly Hindu.

There are also numerous small indigenous tribal groups that make up the rest of the population. The Monpa of the Black Mountains in central Bhutan and the Lhop or Doya of the southwest have recently been identified as the aboriginal population, predating all the other population groups.

A BRIEF HISTORY

The first king of Bhutan, Ugyen Wangchuck.

Until the 1600s, Bhutan existed as a collection of little kingdoms across different valleys in the region, unified only by reverence for the Buddhist saints from Tibet and India. A dual system of governance was established in the mid-seventeenth century, to be replaced in 1907 by the crowning of the first king of Bhutan, Ugyen Wangchuck. Then, after more than a century of security, prosperity, and peace, Bhutan, under the far-sighted leadership of the fourth king, transitioned into a democratic constitutional monarchy in 2008. Bhutan is currently governed by the second elected government.

Down the centuries, Bhutan has been known by multiple names. The people like to call themselves "Drukpa," derived from the name of the country, Druk-Yul or "Land of the Thunder Dragon." The name has its origins in the twelfth century, when the respected Lama Tsangpa Gyare Yeshey Dorje (1161–1211) heard thunder from the direction of Bhutan as he was consecrating a monastery in Tibet.

Bhutan was called other names, including Lho
Jong ("Valleys of the South"), Lho Mon Kha Zhi
("The Southern Country with Four Approaches"), Lho
Jong Men Jong ("The Southern Valleys of Medicinal
Herbs"), and Lho Mon Tsenden Jong ("The Southern
Valleys where Cypress Grows"). The name Bhutan is
believed to be derived from "Bhootan," referring to the
rising lands, by the Indians. Throughout its history,
Bhutan has existed as an independent nation, never
completely conquered or governed by another power.

Early History

Archaeological evidence suggests that Bhutan was
inhabited as long ago as 2000 BCE. Much of Bhutan's
history, however, is strongly tied to Buddhism and the
saints and religious personalities from India and Tibet
who traveled there. Before the arrival of Buddhism, the
inhabitants of Bhutan were mainly nomadic herders
following Bon—an animistic tradition that includes
nature worship. Buddhism firmly established itself
from about the seventh century CE, when the Tibetan
king Songtsen Gampo, who extended his influence as
far as Nepal and Bhutan, built the Kyichu Lhakhang in
Paro and the Jambay Lhakhang in Bumthang—two of
the 108 temples built to pin a demoness down to Earth
in order to enable Buddhism to flourish in Tibet. It is
believed that Kyichu and Jambay Lhakhang hold the
left foot and the left knee of the demoness.

The Bhutanese consider the arrival of one of the
favorite religious figures, the Indian Tantric master
Padmasambhava (known popularly as Guru Rinpoche)

A painting of Tantric master Padmasambhava, or Guru Rinpoche.

in 746 CE as the turning-point in the country's history.
The master was invited by Sendha Gyab (also called
Sindhu Raja), the king of Bumthang, in central Bhutan,
to exorcise demons. Through meditation on the site of
Kurjey—where the main temple of Kurjey Lhakhang
stands today—Guru Rinpoche captured the demons,
resulting in the conversion of the king to Buddhism.

Guru Rinpoche came to Bhutan a second time,
visiting Singye Dzong in Lhuentse and parts of
eastern Bhutan. (A *dzong* is a fortified monastery and
administrative complex unique to Bhutan.) As on his
first visit, he left a body print and impression of his
head with a hat at Gom Kora in Trashiyangtse, where
the monastery stands today. Bhutan's famous Taktsang
monastery (the Tiger's Nest) was the destination of his
flight in the form of Dorji Drolo, one of his eight
manifestations, on the back of a flaming tigress. All
the numerous places Guru Rinpoche visited then are
considered sacred throughout the country, and many
valleys celebrate his great achievements with the
colorful *tshechus* (festivals) described in Chapter 3.

Toward the latter half of the ninth century CE,
Bhutan saw the arrival of Tibetans to settle in eastern
and central Bhutan as a result of persecution at the
hands of the Tibetan king Langdharma, who banished
Buddhism. One of the brothers of the king, Prince
Tsangma, was also banished to Bhutan. A number of
Bhutanese families claim to be descended from him.

In the eleventh century Buddhism was reestablished
in Tibet, with a corresponding increase in pilgrimage
and revival of Buddhist practices in Bhutan. In Tibet,

Lama Tsangpa Gyare Yeshey Dorje established the monastery of Druk and started the lineage of Drukpa Kagyu (also known as Drukpa Kagyupa), which was later to become the state religion of Bhutan.

There was a further significant influx of Tibetans, largely into western Bhutan, at the persecution of the Gelug sect of Buddhism. They established the Drukpa school of Buddhism in Bhutan and saw the growth of different sects within it, including the Lhagpa Kagyu lineage—the followers of Gyalwa Lhanangpa (1164–1224), himself a Tibetan. He built the popular Tango Goemba (monastery) north of Thimphu.

The first half of the thirteenth century saw the arrival of Phajo Drugom Shigpo (1184–1251), belonging to the Drukpa lineage founded in Ralung in Tibet. It is believed that Tsangpa Gyare had prophesied that Phajo would travel to Bhutan and establish the Drukpa school in the southern valleys. Phajo had to compete with the Lhapas to do so, and established the monasteries of Phajoding and Tango in Thimphu. Although Drukpa Kagyu was the dominant school, Bhutan saw many other sects of Buddhism, such as the Barawas, Nyingmapas, and Changzampas. Monasteries belonging to these sects currently exist in Bhutan.

Drukpa Kagyu grew and flourished between the thirteenth and sixteenth centuries with the arrival of more lamas from Ralung, who built more monasteries. The more famous visitors include Lama Ngawang Choegyal (1465–1540), accompanied by his sons, who built a number of monasteries including Druk Choeding in Paro, and Pangri Zampa and Hongtsho in Thimphu. Lama

Drukpa Kuenley, known as the "divine madman," visited Bhutan at the same time, establishing Chimi Lhakhang (known as the "temple of fertility") in Lobesa in Punakha, which is very popular with visitors (see page 78).

While Drukpa Kagyu was flourishing in western Bhutan, Nyingmapa—the oldest sect of Tibetan Buddhism—was flourishing in eastern and central Bhutan. Longchen Rabjampa (1308–63), a Nyingmapa lama, spent his exile in Bumthang, where he established the monasteries of Tharpaling, Samtenling, Shingkhar, and Ugyencholing.

This period was also the era of the treasure hunters, known as the *tertons*, who were prophesied by Guru Rinpoche to discover the sacred texts he hid in caves, rocks, and lakes. The *tertons* were Tantric masters and important religious figures, respected across Bhutan and the Himalayas. The first of the many *tertons*, Dorje Lingpa (1346–1405), came to Bhutan from Tibet and settled in the Chakhar and Ugyencholing Valleys of Bumthang

The best known of all the *tertons*, Pema Lingpa (1450–1521), was born in the Tang Valley in Bumthang, and was believed to be the reincarnation of Guru Rinpoche and Longchen Rabjampa. He recovered his first *terma*, or treasure, from the lake of Membartsho ("the burning lake") in Bumthang in 1725. He also founded the monasteries of Petsheling, Kunzangdra, and Tamshing in Bumthang, and crafted numerous sacred dances based on his visions.

The influence of these Buddhist masters extends through the parts played by their descendants in establishing strongholds of religion and many ruling clans and families, who continue to play significant roles into the modern era.

Bhutan continued to remain a collection of small communities until the arrival of the Zhabdrung Ngawang Namgyal in 1616 from Ralung, who later went on to unify the country.

The Zhabdrung Era, 1600–1907

The monastery built by Tsangpa Gyare at Ralung became the main seat of the Drukpa Kagyu school, with their subsequent hierarchs recognized as the heads of the Drukpa Kagyu school, called the Drukchen. This lineage was to play a dominant role in shaping Bhutan generally from 1600 to the establishment of the monarchy in 1907.

The reincarnation of Tsangpa Gyare, Kunga Peljor, was born into the ruling family of Ralung, with the subsequent reincarnations, Jamyang Chodrak and Pema Karpo, being born outside the ruling family. Pema Karpo is considered the most illustrious Drukpa scholar, writing a significant quantity of texts on Buddhist philosophy, astrology, and history.

After the death of Pema Karpo in 1592, Ngawang Namgyal, of the princely Gya family, was enthroned as the eighteenth abbot of Ralung. He was recognized as the reincarnation of Pema Karpo, but this was challenged by the Tsang Desi, ruler of Upper Tsang in Tibet based at Zhigatse. The Tsang Desi had his own candidate, Pagsam Wangpo, who was enthroned as the head of the Drukpa school. Negotiations were undertaken to reconcile the matter, but Ngawang Namgyal was forced into exile. He looked to the country of Bhutan, which his forefathers had visited before him. His great-grandfather Ngagi Wangchuck and his father Tenpye Nyima had built monasteries in the center and east of the country.

Ngawang Namgyal accepted the invitation of the followers of the Drukpa school, firmly established since the thirteenth century, and sought refuge in western Bhutan. He fled from Ralung in 1616, carrying with him the precious image of Rangjung Kharsapani that is believed to have emanated from of the first vertebra of Tsangpa Gyare. Supported by Tendzin Drugye, a Bhutanese monk in Ralung, Ngawang Namgyal fled south to Laya and to Pangri Zampa in Thimphu, finally seeking refuge in Paro at Druk Choeding, and subsequently became Zhabdrung, the title he assumed in Bhutan.

The Drukpa State of Bhutan

Before the Zhabdrung could consolidate the Drukpa state of Bhutan, he had to fight against enemies from abroad and within Bhutan. Shortly after his departure from Tibet, the Tsang Desi Phuntshok Namgyel sent an army to fight him at Paro. The Zhabdrung was able to repel the invasion, and following the victory, he forged an alliance with Tshewang Tenzing, grandson of Drukpa Kuenley, at Tango. In 1620 the Zhabdrung built the Cheri monastery, and also built a stupa (shrine;

these are generally dome-shaped) to hold the ashes of his deceased father. With the alliances and the victory, the Zhabdrung was beginning to be seen as a leader, allowing him to enter into diplomatic relations with the neighboring kingdom of Cooch Behar, now in India.

As Drukpa Kagyu began to grow, the Zhabdrung resolved in 1626 to establish a unified system of governance, combining both spiritual and temporal authority. To start building cohesion, he decided to build the Simtokha Dzong, the construction of which was opposed by the "five groups of lamas"—heads of the sects of schools already established in Bhutan. The Zhabdrung successfully fought against them, completing the construction of the castle monastery of Simtokha Dzong in 1629, and establishing firm control of the political and religious powers in western Bhutan.

The Tibetan attacks were not over. There were subsequent invasions in 1634 and 1639, with little success. In 1639, the Tsang Desi fought with assistance from the Lam Kha Ngas. In 1640, the enth Karmapa and many other senior Tibetan lamas mediated to resolve the reincarnation issue at Ralung. Accordingly, Pagsam Wangpo was recognized as the Drukchen at Ralung and the Zhabdrung as the supreme authority of the southern country of Mon.

In 1645 and 1649 Bhutan came into further conflict with its northern neighbors, now a combined force of Tibetans and Mongols, after the fall of the Tsang Desi to the Mongol armies of Gushi Qan in 1642. However, the Zhabdrung prevailed in both these battles. Following the battle in 1649, the Drukgyal Dzong was built to celebrate the triumph over the Tibetans. By 1649, the Zhabdrung had effectively unified western Bhutan under his control.

Choesi: The Dual System of Governance

The Zhabdrung introduced the code of spiritual and temporal law in Bhutan, which was based on the Tibetan systems. The tenth Je Khenpo (chief abbot), Tendzin Choegyal, committed it to writing in 1729, until which time it had been transmitted orally. The Zhabdrung wanted Bhutan's religious and cultural identity to be different from those of Tibet. He also instituted a system of taxes, which were to be paid in kind in the form of animal or farm produce—such as wheat, rice, buckwheat, butter, or timber—or clothing. Families were required to contribute labor to the construction of paths, *dzongs*, temples, and bridges— a practice that was to continue until its elimination by the third king.

In the 1640s the Zhabdrung introduced the system of Choesi, which separated the administration of the country into two offices, religious and secular. The religious and spiritual aspects were to be headed by the Je Khenpo and the political, administrative, and secular affairs were to be handled by the Druk Desi.

Having consolidated western Bhutan, Zhabdrung entered into solitary retreat in Punakha Dzong, where he died. Many believe that this was in 1651, and that he passed away on the tenth day of the third

Bhutanese month (May in the Gregorian calendar). His death was kept secret for the next fifty-eight years, until 1708, in the interest of national security.

The Choesi system was to last until 1907, during which time Bhutan saw fifty-five Druk Desis. The tradition of the Je Khenpo still continues in Bhutan, and the current one is the seventieth Je Khenpo in the tradition established by the Zhabdrung in 1633. Most of the Desis were either political monks or descendants of prominent families. As eastern and central Bhutan were brought under Drukpa rule, the Desi was supported by the Penlops and Dzongpons—the powerful regional governors of Paro, Trongsa, Daga, Punakha, Thimphu, and Wangduephodrang.

Between 1651 and 1708, when Zhabdrung's death was finally announced, Bhutan saw a period of stability under four successive Desis who were closely linked to the Zhabdrung, and ensured stability and continued consolidation of the country. The first Druk Desi, Bhutanese by birth, had accompanied the Zhabdrung during his flight from Tibet. He established the *driglam-namzha* (see page 54), the national code of conduct that cemented Bhutan's distinct identity and culture. He was also responsible for bringing eastern and central Bhutan under Drukpa rule.

The second Druk Desi was the half brother of Zhabdrung who promoted the classical sciences, arts, and crafts, and built Drukgyal and Ta Dzongs in Paro. The third Druk Desi, also close to the Zhabdrung, oversaw a number of important Buddhist works in the country, including the completion of eight gilt sandalwood stupas in Punakha and the renovation of Simtokha Dzong. It was during this period that Bhutan's influence extended elsewhere to Sikkim, Kalimpong, Ladakh, and other places in Tibet and Nepal.

The fourth Druk Desi, brought up by the Zhabdrung as crown prince, was spiritually much respected; he helped to expand the monastic community in Punakha and introduced sacred dances that a performed during festivals in Bhutan. He also built a number of important buildings and monasteries, such as the Ha Damsang Dzong, Taktsang in Paro, and Tango in Thimphu.

Political Instability and Internal Strife

The next two hundred years, until the establishment of the monarchy in 1907, were the most unstable in the history of Bhutan, with civil wars, internal conflicts, and political infighting. Most reincarnations of the Zhabdrung were politically weak and unable to demonstrate the charisma and leadership necessary to bring the country together. To be a Druk Desi during this period was dangerous. Twenty-two Druk Desis were either assassinated or quickly deposed by rivals during these years, with the exception of the thirteenth Desi Sherub Wangchuck, who ruled for twenty years.

The political situation enabled rival factions to appeal to the Tibetans for assistance, and even to go as far as Beijing to ask the Chinese emperor for mediation. As a result, Bhutan was invaded by Tibet in 1729 and

1730. In fact between 1651 and 1730, Bhutan was invaded around seven times by Tibet. In addition to establishing alliances with the Panchen Lama in Tibet, Bhutan also looked south in the 1730s, coming into conflict with Cooch Behar and establishing alliances with King Prithvi Narayan Shah of Nepal.

It was Bhutan's involvement in the succession matters of the kingdom of Cooch Behar in 1765, during the rule of the fifteenth Druk Desi, Tendzing, that would bring the Bhutanese into contact with the British East India Company. The claimants to the throne of Cooch Behar sought military assistance from the British East India Company, who defeated the Bhutanese and took possession of the border areas of Cooch Behar and southern Bhutan. Subsequent missions were to follow into Bhutan to broker preferential trade agreements in Bhutan. The missions were led by George Bogle in 1774, Alexander Hamilton in 1776–77, and Samuel Turner in 1783, during which there were good relations.

The Duar War
However, between 1830 and 1864 the relationship between Bhutan and British India turned hostile over the Bengal Duars, a narrow stretch of fertile flood plain in the southern foothills that was under Bhutanese control. The situation worsened when, in 1864, the Bhutanese humiliated a British mission led by Ashley Eden, and demanded the unconditional return of all the Duars (the Assam Duars were by then already under the control of British India). Eventually,

in November 1864, war broke out. The Duar War lasted for five months, and ended with the Treaty of Sinchula, restoring friendly relations between Bhutan and British India, and with Bhutan agreeing to the permanent annexation of the Duars and Kalimpong by the British. Bhutan received some monetary compensation in exchange, and is believed to do so even today from India.

During this period the central government had significantly weakened, resulting in central and eastern Bhutan coming under the control of Trongsa's *penlop* (governor), Jigme Namgyal (1825–81). On his death he was succeeded by his son, Ugyen Wangchuck, who further increased his power by seizing the Simtokha Dzong and the Trashichho Dzong. He also defeated his rivals in the decisive victory of the battle of Changlimithang in 1885, establishing himself as the de facto ruler of the country.

Ugyen Wangchuck wished to extend the relationship with the British, and acted as an intermediary between the British and Tibet, helping the Younghusband Mission to Tibet in 1904. In return he was awarded the title of Knight Commander of the Indian Empire (KCIE) in 1906.

Having established an unassailable position as leader and a credible relationship with the neighbors, particularly with British India, Ugyen Wangchuck was elected by an assembly of representatives of the monastic community, civil servants, and the people, as the first hereditary king of Bhutan on December 17, 1907. This brought to end the Choesi, the dual system of governance established by Zhabdrung Ngawang Namgyal.

The Monarchy: 1907–Present

King Ugyen Wangchuck continued to maintain excellent relationships with P   ish India. In 1910, Bhutan and British India signed the Treaty of Punakha, allowing the British government to advise Bhutan on external affairs while not interfering in its internal affairs. This meant that Bhutan had to consult the British on any matters related to disputes with neighbors, such as Sikkim and Cooch Behar. The British also doubled the compensation for the Duars to 100,000 Indian rupees a year. However, Bhutan did not agree to allow a permanent British Resident (diplomatic advisor) in Bhutan.

When Ugyen Wangchuck died in 1926 he was succeeded by his son, Jigme Wangchuck, who ruled until 1952. Although the world was ravaged initially by the depression in the 1930s and subsequently by the Second World War, Bhutan was not significantly affected as a result of its self-imposed isolation and nascent economy. As in the period of Ugyen Wangchuck's rule, Bhutan saw political stability and some economic prosperity. In addition to establishing the palaces of Kunga Rabten and Wangdi Choling in Bumthang, Jigme Wangchuck is credited with bringing modern education to Bhutan. He also sent selected young Bhutanese to study in India. In 1949, he negotiated the Indo–Bhutan Treaty with independent India, reinforcing Bhutan's sovereignty and independence. While India agreed not to interfere in the internal affairs of Bhutan, Bhutan agreed to be guided by India in its external affairs.

Although Bhutan saw glimpses of modernization to come, it was not until the reign of the third king, Jigme

Dorji Wangchuck, fondly known as the Father of Modern Bhutan, that development began in earnest in Bhutan.

Jigme Dorji Wangchuck succeeded to the throne in 1952 on the death of his father. The third king was educated in India and in England, and brought in a deep understanding and wider view of the world from political and economic perspectives. He began to sow the seeds of democracy in Bhutan by establishing the national assembly (Tshogdu) in 1953, and formulating a new legal and judicial system. He modernized the army and the police force, and abolished serfdom in Bhutan. (Serfdom had developed in the early nineteenth century when people were brought into the country in droves from India to work in the fields, and over time became "unfree labor," bonded for generations to wealthy families doing menial jobs.)

The third king viewed diplomatic relationships and a presence on the world stage as integral to Bhutan's sovereignty and independence, and in 1958 invited the prime minister of India, Jawaharlal Nehru, to Bhutan. His view was reinforced when China took control of Tibet in that year.

Bhutan joined a number of international bodies during his reign, beginning with the membership of the Colombo Plan in 1961, Universal Postal Union in 1969, and culminating with the United Nations in 1971. Under his rule, Bhutan also started the first "five-year plan" in 1961 with the assistance of India, which included building roads and the Chukha Hydroelectric project.

The fourth king of Bhutan, Jigme Singye Wangchuck, ascended the throne in 1974 at the tender age of seventeen, after his father's death. His focus has been on driving socioeconomic development, with the goal of achieving self-reliance while preserving tradition, culture, and the national environment. While continuing the economic activities and the plan that his father initiated, he established relationships with a number of countries, including Japan, Norway, the European Union, and Switzerland. Bhutan also became a member of many international organizations, such as the Non-Aligned Movement, SAARC, ADB, the World Bank, and the IMF.

During the period leading up to the introduction of democracy in 2008, Bhutan had to face two major problems in the south of the country. Prior to the twentieth century, a small number of ethnic Nepalis started settling in the inhospitable terrain in the south. Their numbers grew as Bhutan began to develop, and many were granted Bhutanese nationality in 1958. Further development brought an increased influx of migrants, and following the census of 1988, those people who did not have citizenship were declared illegal immigrants and deported. It is alleged that about 80,000 of them went to refugee camps in Nepal, and, despite a series of negotiations between the governments of Bhutan and Nepal, a resolution has not been reached. Following an agreement between the UNHCR and some Western governments in 2008, the refugees are in the process of resettling in North America, Europe, and other Western countries.

The other problem that Bhutan had to contend with was the eviction of the Indian separatist groups of Bodo and ULFA, who had set up camps in the jungles of southern Bhutan. In 2003, following the failure of negotiations with the militants, the fourth king led an operation with the army and successfully expelled the insurgents from Bhutan.

The fourth king is also known globally for pioneering the use of happiness in the form of Gross National Happiness (GNH), instead of Gross Domestic Product, as the yardstick for development. GNH is more broadly discussed on page 51.

BHUTAN TODAY

In 2005, the king announced plans to abdicate in favor of the crown prince, Jigme Khesar Namgyel Wangchuck, and move the country from an Absolute Monarchy to a democratic Constitutional Monarchy in 2008. The king, through a committee of senior government officials, drafted the constitution and traveled around the country, talking to and gathering input from the people. The Constitution of the Kingdom of Bhutan, formally adopted on July 18, 2008, is the Supreme Law of the country.

Under Jigme Khesar Namgyel Wangchuck, Bhutan has seen significant investment in hydroelectricity and economic development.

The political transition to democracy was unique, as it was the fourth king of Bhutan who initiated and

A roadside portrait of King Jigme Khesar Namgyel Wangchuck and Queen Jetsun Pema.

guided the democratization process, in contrast to many other countries around the world where democracy was pursued by popular movements. For Bhutan and its people, democracy was bestowed upon them by the Throne. As the country takes careful steps forward, the people of Bhutan continue to look to their king for guidance and direction.

GOVERNMENT AND JUDICIARY

The year 2008 is the most significant year in modern Bhutanese history. The country became a constitutional monarchy, with the king as the head of state and an elected prime minister as the head of the government, a change made under the direction of the fourth king.

The Parliament of Bhutan has two houses: the upper
house, called the National Council, and the Lower
House, called the National Assembly. The National
Council, which replaced the old Royal Advisory
Council, has twenty-five non-partisan members. Of
these, five are nominated by the king on account of
their contribution and status, and twenty are elected
by the people, one for each of the twenty *dzongkhags*
(districts), for a five-year term.

The National Assembly has forty-seven members
(*thumi)* elected through their constituencies on a first-
past-the-post system. The leader of the ruling party
becomes the prime minister, and he is supported by
his ten cabinet ministers. In addition, the government
works with a number of other autonomous agencies
such as the Anti-Corruption Commission, the Royal
Monetary Authority, the Civil Service Commission,
and the Audit Authority.

Each district has a district government headed
by a district governor or commissioners called the
dzongda. They are appointed by the king on the
recommendation of the prime minister, and are
responsible for developing and delivering the plans
for the district. Some districts may have sub-districts
called the *dungkhags*, which will have a sub-district
administrator (*dungpa*). At the block level, the village
headman is the administrative officer, elected by the
community for a period of three years. They look after
developmental activities assisted by a civil servant.

The Bhutanese legal system has its roots in a set
of laws and codes based closely on the Buddhist

principles propagated by Zhabdrung Ngawang Namgyal in the mid-1600s and addressing the violation of both spiritual and temporal laws. In 1959, under the guidance of the third king, the first comprehensive codified law code, the *Thrimzhung Chhenmo* or the Supreme Law, was established. In 2001 the Civil and Criminal Procedure Code, which contains rules and regulations dealing with court procedure, was passed. In 2004 the fourth king abolished capital punishment and instated a revised Penal Code of Bhutan.

The Supreme Court is the highest in the four-tier court system, followed by the High Court, the Dzongkhag courts, and the Dungkhag courts. There are no courts or tribunals of special jurisdiction in Bhutan. However, other courts and tribunals may be established when necessary by the king on the recommendation of the National Judicial Commission. Every Bhutanese has access to the king, to whom all Bhutanese may appeal.

THE ECONOMY

Between 50 and 60 percent of Bhutanese are still engaged in agriculture—mainly subsistence farming and animal husbandry. Major sectors of the economy today consist of forestry, tourism, and the sale of hydroelectric power.

The Bhutanese currency, the Bhutanese ngultrum (Nu.), is at par with the Indian rupee. Bhutan has one

of the world's smallest economies, with the 2019 Gross Domestic Product at about US $2.8bn. An average GDP growth rate of 7 to 10 percent, driven largely by hydroelectricity and the construction sector, has slowed to 5 to 7 percent in recent years.

In order to become self-sufficient, Bhutan has been investing heavily in hydroelectricity, with assistance from India. Tourism is another important component of the economy, with over 250,000 visitors arriving annually. While the coronovarius pandemic of 2020 saw the industry grind to a halt as the country sealed its borders to help contain the spread of the virus, visitor numbers are expected to slowly return to pre-pandemic levels upon reopening. The industry's recovery is critical as it is through tourism that Bhutan generates significant foreign currency, in addition to providing employment to over 50,000 people.

There are small-scale industries focused on the manufacturing of cement, steel, and other materials, and the processing of minerals for export. The financial services sector is evolving, with four major banks and multiple insurance companies. It also has a fledgling stock exchange on which local companies are listed.

Bhutan's economy is not without challenges. It is well known for being narrow and overly dependent on a few sectors. In order to address this issue, the government has been actively encouraging the development of other sectors, such as waste management, education services, and information technology. In addition, there has been a deliberate focus on attracting foreign investment through FDI into a number of sectors.

Another feature of the economy is the increasing reliance on external debts to fund the massive hydroelectricity projects. The debt to GDP ratio currently stands at 110 percent. While many worry about the unsustainability of the debts and risks to the wider economy, the government is confident that the debts are self-liquidating.

A key challenge is rising unemployment, particularly among the young, and the attendant risk of social instability. With youth unemployment at roughly 10 percent, the government has been implementing various schemes to support young people to help them broaden their skills, and identify avenues for employment.

BHUTAN IN THE WORLD

Bhutan has a good standing in the world and has shown leadership across a number of areas. It is generally credited as the first country to focus on improving the happiness and wellbeing of its people, moving away from the traditional emphasis on material progress. While Bhutan reports economic growth, the primary measure used by the government and the people is the Gross National Happiness indicator.

The GNH measure is used to identify improvement across multiple areas, such as quality of life, education, health, tradition and culture, and the environment. Bhutan has been able to inspire many countries (such as the UK, France, and Brazil) and organizations (the UN, the World Bank) to consider measuring wellbeing to develop policies and intervention.

Bhutan is well known for demonstrating leadership in the preservation of the environment. Through the stewardship of its kings, it has maintained significant forest cover, provided safe habitat for endangered species, and adopted many environmentally friendly and sustainable policies. As already noted, Bhutan is the only carbon-negative country in the world.

Finally, Bhutan is seen as a country that is genuinely proud of its culture and traditions, and many visitors come to experience this way of life, which in many ways remains untouched by the material needs of the modern world.

CHAPTER TWO

VALUES &
ATTITUDES

THE BUDDHIST WAY OF LIFE

As we have seen in Chapter 1, the history of Bhutan is entwined with the advent of Tantric Buddhism (as Tibetan Buddhism is popularly known in the West) in the eighth century. Since then, this has been the defining feature of the Bhutanese people, except in the south, where Hinduism predominates.

Buddhism plays a pivotal role in everyday life in Bhutan, and Buddhist belief permeates daily habits and practices. Each day begins with the offerings of water and prayers at the altar in every household's dedicated shrine room. Water is a universal offering, representing whatever what one wishes to share, such as food or drink. Astrologers are consulted and divine intervention is sought before any important decisions are made or actions taken. A person will rarely start an activity such as an exam, a job interview, or a long journey without a visit to the local monastery, and anyone preparing to go to the hospital for treatment will undergo a religious ritual, or *rimdoe*, performed at home. Every stage of life—birth, marriage, death, and everything in between—is shaped by Buddhist belief.

MONARCHY AND NATIONAL IDENTITY

Of all the institutions in Bhutan, the monarchy is the paramount symbol of national identity. Established in 1907 after a tumultuous period of internecine wars among chieftains and clans across the country, Bhutan's hereditary monarchical system has led it through a century of peace, prosperity, and modern development.

The Bhutanese have immense love and respect for their king and the royal family. They like to talk about them, and about the blessings they have brought the people of Bhutan over the last century. They proudly display big pictures of the king, queen, and members of the royal family in their sitting rooms and at the altar in their shrine rooms, alongside statues of Buddha, other Buddhist deities, and Buddhist masters. The Bhutanese enjoy celebrating events related to the king, and it is common for him and the royal family members to participate in these and to interact with the people. Every year, the king travels to a different district in the country to celebrate Bhutan's National Day (December 17) with the people. Villagers from far and wide come together to take part, and particularly to see their beloved king in person.

GROSS NATIONAL HAPPINESS

Some decades ago, few people knew anything about Bhutan. Now probably most of the world has heard of it because of GNH, or Gross National Happiness.

Happiness and life satisfaction have always been a part of Buddhism, but the present approach in Bhutan originated in the wisdom of the fourth king. His recognition that raising the "per capita income" would not by itself improve the happiness of the people of Bhutan—which includes political stability, social harmony, and the Bhutanese culture and way of life—gave rise to his comment to the London *Financial Times* that "Gross National Happiness (GNH) is more important than Gross Domestic Product (GDP)."

The Bhutanese are happy people, full of optimism. While economic development is seen as important, the focus of both the government and the people is on the pursuit of a happy, fulfilling life. The Bhutanese strive for balance in their lives, with wellbeing as the key goal.

GNH, the sole objective of which is to increase the overall happiness and wellbeing of society, now guides much of what Bhutan does. All government policies are required to be aligned to key tenets of GNH, which include ensuring economic growth, preservation of culture and tradition, environmental conservation, and good governance. School curricula are also designed to align with the principles of Gross National Happiness.

This is the dominant perception of many Bhutanese, particularly of those who live and work in the urban areas, and you will be surprised by how passionately people talk about GNH—it makes for a great conversation starter!

WHAT IS GROSS NATIONAL HAPPINESS?

GNH is evaluated by using a combination of four pillars: economic growth, cultural preservation, ecological protection, and good governance with no corruption. These four pillars have been expanded into nine domains: standard of living, good governance, time use and balance, community vitality, cultural diversity and resilience, ecosystem diversity and resilience, health of the population, education, and psychological wellbeing.

The Centre for Bhutan Studies—a Bhutan-based think tank—has also developed thirty-three criteria based on national public opinion surveys to measure the progress toward national wellbeing as reflected in the nine domains. Ultimately, at the center of all development efforts under GNH is a focus on the material and spiritual welfare and wellbeing of each individual in Bhutan.

INTERDEPENDENCE

The Bhutanese people are strongly influenced by the Buddhist concept of interdependence—the idea that all phenomena are connected through cause and effect. They carefully consider the impact of their actions on the wider society, the environment, and their personal *karma*. This is evident in various ways, such as in the great openness and hospitality shown throughout the country, and in the display of compassion toward all sentient beings. This has allowed the government to generate support for its approach to development—the Gross National Happiness—particularly around the preservation of the natural environment.

THA-DAMTSI AND *LEY-JUMDREY*

Two other beliefs that are strongly related to the concept of interdependence are *tha-damtsi* and *ley-jumdrey*.

Tha-damtsi means the loyalty of the Bhutanese people to the king, the country, and the people. The Bhutanese are a proud people, and the display of *tha-damtsi* is considered integral and paramount in preserving Bhutan's unique identity, distinct culture, and traditions, and in extending Bhutan's sovereignty.

Ley-jumdrey refers to the law of cause and effect, or *karma*. The Bhutanese believe that the circumstances of one's current life are the outcome of one's deeds and actions in one's past lives as well as in this life. Every activity that an individual undertakes will affect not only the current life but also the future lives. Although the accumulation of merits through everyday actions and behavior is important for all, it becomes a major preoccupation for the elderly, who spend most of their time praying, circumambulating monasteries or stupas, and going on pilgrimages. This is often reflected in the accepting attitude of the Bhutanese, who, when confronted with a difficult situation in life, endure it with equanimity.

Tha-damtsi and *ley-jumdrey* are the fundamental pillars that ensure social harmony and individual conduct, and are taught in schools, at home, and at workplaces as part of *driglam-namzha*—a set code of conduct and cultural etiquette.

DRIGLAM-NAMZHA

While the concepts of *tha-damtsi* and *ley-jumdrey* may be difficult to grasp, one could argue that *driglam-namzha* brings aspects of them to life. *Driglam-namzha* refers to one's personal conduct, the display of good manners—physically, verbally and mentally—and avoidance of bad habits unbecoming to a cultured person, whether alone or in the company of other people. The practice of *driglam-namzha* is considered and celebrated as a marker of Bhutanese culture and identity, and every Bhutanese is expected to have some fundamental understanding of it. A person who can demonstrate a good understanding and practice of *driglam-namzha* can expect to get far in Bhutan.

The norms and practices of *driglam-namzha* go back to Buddhist practices in the monasteries, and were codified in the seventeenth century by Zhabdrung Ngawang Namgyal when he instituted the dual system of governance in Bhutan. After the Royal Decree in 1989, *driglam-namzha* has become an official protocol, with a set code of ceremonial conduct that is strictly followed within the government service, and training is provided throughout schooling and before entering the civil service. However, some may argue that the practice is an authoritarian imposition to reinforce hierarchy and the existing social structure, and that there is an element of making sure that people "know their place."

HARMONY WITH NATURE

One of the key pillars of Gross National Happiness is ecological protection, and this is not accidental. Respect for nature and the environment is very much a part of the Buddhist way of living. Mountaineering is not allowed in Bhutan, as the high mountains are believed to be the abode of local deities, and climbing them would be considered sacrilegious. Likewise, pristine lakes are believed to be the abode of the spirits. Visitors are strictly warned against swimming in them, or polluting them by bringing meat anywhere near them or by leaving garbage behind. There are stories of people getting sick or losing their way with the sudden rise of a strong mist from a lake, making it impossible to see, which is thought to show the spirits' displeasure.

The Bhutanese living in rural areas who rely on agriculture, through Buddhist beliefs and also through advocacy from the government, recognize the importance of the ecosystem, and every activity they undertake ensures that they are in harmony with nature. Where big changes to topography have to be made—for example, for infrastructure projects—these are preceded by an environmental impact assessment and with rituals and offerings to appease the local spirits and deities. The Bhutanese take pride in their record of environmental protection and conservation, and Bhutan is seen as a global leader in this area.

BELIEFS AND SUPERSTITIONS

Beliefs and superstitions arising out of Buddhist traditions and reverence for nature play a significant role in everyday life. It is customary for an individual to seek guidance from an astrologer or to consult their *zakar* (daily horoscope) before undertaking any major activities such as getting married, offering or accepting a promotion, venturing on a long journey, or moving to a new house. The day and the exact time are planned. Sometimes, when options are not available, extensive prayers are performed to remove obstacles and bad fortune. Zealous individuals go a step further, even deciding on a favorable day to have a haircut or cut their fingernails.

It is common practice to roll dice for guidance when visiting monasteries. A pair of dice is held on the forehead in prayers for your wish and then thrown on to a tray in front of the altar. The monk counts the number shown and reads the answer from a book.

FAMILY VALUES

Families are generally close knit. Traditionally, Bhutanese families rely on and support each other during times of need. The social support system is still

rudimentary, and poor—perhaps unemployed—relatives will look to the more successful family members for support, financial or otherwise. It is common for elderly parents to live with their children, and they often stay at home to look after their grandchildren. As Bhutan develops, this attitude is changing, especially in the towns. There are more incidences of homelessness, often worsened by the rising unemployment.

We can safely say that in Bhutan, among the northern Drukpa community, both parents play vital and equal roles as the heads of the family, working together in running the household and making key decisions. Elders in the family command respect, and their approval of important decisions is always sought and welcomed. In the southern Lhotshampa community, who are mostly Hindus, family hierarchy exists, and the father is the patriarch.

ATTITUDES TOWARD WOMEN

There is no legal or overt discrimination against women in Bhutanese culture. Women in Bhutan enjoy significant equality compared to their counterparts in the neighboring countries. Men and women work equally hard, alongside each other, whether in offices, towns, or out in the fields.

There is no preference for a boy in the family. Abortion is, however, illegal, and is a sensitive issue. But this stems from the Buddhist belief in not harming a living being, rather than from a social concern about female infanticide, which is an issue in some countries. Women have equal freedom of choice of marriage partners, and they keep their maiden name after marriage. In fact, the western Ngalop are a matriarchal society, where the mother is the head of the family and the daughters inherit all the family wealth; the sons must fend for themselves.

Divorce is common, especially in the urban areas. The law allows young children under the age of nine to remain with the mother, and the father provides a monthly allowance. It doesn't matter who initiates the divorce or who is at fault, unless the court finds compelling reasons to order otherwise. When the children have reached the age of nine they can decide whether to remain with their mother or to live with their father. For Bhutanese women being a divorcée or a widow is not a taboo. A widow can choose to remarry with full support from her family.

SEXUAL MORES

Bhutan has always been seen as a liberal society and the Bhutanese are fairly easygoing when it comes to attitudes toward sex, although you may not find sex-related topics discussed openly around the dining table. Women and men have an equal right to choose their partners, and engaging in sexual relationships before marriage is not frowned upon. "Night hunting" (as described on page 118), when a man enters a potential partner's house at night, is considered a form of courtship—a liberal concept even by any Western measure.

While homosexuality is not a topic you will find discussed openly, there is very little discrimination against gays or lesbians in Bhutan. The Bhutanese in general have an accepting attitude, and they regard what a person does privately as a personal matter.

RESPECT AND HUMILITY

Showing respect is an integral part of being Bhutanese. As in the neighboring countries, showing respect to elders and superiors is important and deeply engrained in people's attitudes.

When addressing someone, you don't use their first name unless they are a close friend. If the person is perceived to be older than you, he or she is addressed as *Aue*, an interchangeable term meaning "Elder Brother" or "Elder Sister." Children would often address strangers as "Auntie" or "Uncle" to show respect.

Success, wealth, and status in society also command respect. The terms *Aum* for women and *Dasho* for men are used to address them. It may surprise you as a visitor when everybody calls you "Sir" or "Madam," and you might also find that this is used in combination with your own name, as in "Sir John," whether you have a knighthood or not!

A straightforward "no" is considered rude, especially if someone in need asks you a favor. The

person asked might choose to go out of his or her way to fulfill the request rather than say a simple "no." It can be frustrating and difficult for Westerners, however, when answers to questions are vague or evaded altogether.

When you are sitting down, never cross your feet or legs, as this is considered disrespectful. Keep your legs close together, with your hands resting on your lap.

It is considered bad manners if you appear very opinionated and sure of yourself. Humility is expected, and considered to come naturally to an individual. In Bhutan, the confident posture seen as normal in the West would be regarded as arrogant, and frowned upon. (See page 187.)

EDUCATION

In the past it was common for every Bhutanese family
to send their young sons to the local monastery to
attend Buddhist training and become monks. As
Bhutan embarked on modern development, this
practice, although still continuing, has declined over
the years. It has notably been observed that most of
the children joining monastic schools at a young age
are from poor or disadvantaged backgrounds.

Modern education is now firmly seen as a way to
improve one's life in Bhutan. Whereas the government
used to have to force people to send their children to
school, every family now wants their children to have
an education. This is further encouraged by the
government, which provides free education to every

child of school age. It also provides university scholarships to students who excel in their exams. Parents take pride in their children's performance at school, and this is usually a major topic of discussion at gatherings.

For most Bhutanese, a job in the civil service is still the ultimate career goal, as such positions bring respect and prestige.

The Bhutanese turn to the private sector for job opportunities when all else has failed. The private sector is still in its infancy, and, though developing, is not generally seen as a sector that provides better job opportunities.

TRADITIONAL DRESS

Bhutan's national dress is considered very important in the preservation of the country's distinct culture and national identity. People take great pride in their national dress. They regularly wear it to the office and on occasions such as visits to monasteries and *dzongs*, and children wear it to school. The dress for men is called a *gho* (pronounced "go"), which is similar to the Tibetan *chuba*, but more "pulled together" in appearance. The *gho* is a gown-like dress, hoisted knee length, and tied around the waist with a hand-woven belt called a *kera* (not to be confused with the women's garment, the *kira*). Under the *gho*, men wear a jacket called a *tegu*, with long, folded-back cuffs.

Women wear a *kira*, a rectangular piece of cloth measuring about 100 inches by 60 inches (2.5 by 1.5 m), which is wound around the body and held together by a *koma* (a beautifully designed metal clasp) over the shoulders and tied neatly at the waist. The floor-length *kira* is usually accompanied by a blouse, called a *wonju,* and an outer jacket, a *teogo.* They are mostly handwoven with intricate designs. The modified version of the *kira*, a wrap-around skirt, has become popular now as it is deemed easier to wear. These large cloths often come in handy for blankets while traveling.

The textiles all used to be designed and handwoven by talented weavers around the country. While the art of weaving is still alive and appreciated, cheaper, factory-made imports from India have flooded the market in recent years. These are useful for everyday wear, but the expensive, locally handwoven fabrics are the first choice when it comes to choosing dresses for special occasions such as festivals and weddings. The intricate weaves are passed down as family heirlooms, preserved and much loved through generations. A wedding dress is carefully chosen based on the design and color most favorable to the individual, taking astrological predictions into account.

Some of the highland communities, like the Brokpas and the Layaps, wear their own distinctive costumes made from sheep's and yak's wool.

Ceremonial Scarves: *Kabney*, *Patang*, and *Rachu*

Bhutan is a hierarchical society defined by rank and position within the civil service or one's standing in society. One of the indications of this is the use of ceremonial scarves. The scarf for men is called a *kabney*, and the scarf for women is called a *rachu*; both are worn draped over the left shoulder.

Both *kabney* and *rachu* are used for official occasions such as going to a *dzong*, entering buildings with the national flag, and on special occasions such as weddings or official ceremonies. Depending on the color of the scarf, you can identify its wearer's status, particularly in the case of a man. The king wears a yellow *kabney*, a minister an orange, while a commoner would wear a white tasseled scarf. The red scarf is conferred by the king on a deserving individual for his or her achievements (along with the title of Dasho, which is equivalent to a knighthood in the UK). All high-ranking officials also wear a decorative sword called a *patang*.

A woman's *rachu* is folded lengthwise and worn over the left shoulder. Only the members of the Royal Family drape the full-length *rachu* (broader in size and intricately designed) over both shoulders with the ends placed neatly in front. The common *rachu* is a simple design with multiple stripes on a maroon background called *ada rachu*.

Scarf Hierarchy and Colors
Yellow: His Majesty the King / Je Khenpo, chief abbot
Orange: Minister / deputy minister / opposition leader / chairman of the national council
Indigo Blue: Member of parliament
Red: Dasho, conferred by the king
Green: Judge / *drangpons* (associated justice)
White tassel and red stripes: Village head / district administrator
Plain white tassel: Commoner (male)

ATTITUDES TOWARD FOOD

Food is an important part of everyday life in Bhutan. Relationships and family time are often organized and built around meals. The Bhutanese are extremely mindful of the need for hospitality, and make sure to provide the best they can in terms of food and drink when guests come visiting. The giving of food is also an important aspect of Buddhism, and religious festivals and ceremonies incorporate food offerings (discussed in Chapter 3), a meritorious act that teaches one to be selfless and giving, and to care for the needs of others.

The Bhutanese are largely non-vegetarian, and enjoy a variety of meat, fish, and poultry, but this is changing. Over the last decade there has been a shift, especially among the younger generation, away from the consumption of meat and meat products. This, besides being a choice for health reasons, is also on grounds of Buddhism—showing compassion toward all sentient beings and refraining from harming animals. Many people abstain from eating meat on specific religious days, and during the auspicious Buddhist months of *Dawai Dangpa* (first month) and *Dawai Zhipa* (fourth month) there is a total ban on selling meat throughout the country. For visitors, hotels usually stock up on meat when it is available.

SHARING AND GIVING

Thuenlam, or maintaining and fostering relationships, is important for the Bhutanese—whether between boss and subordinate, teacher and student; or with neighbors, family, and friends. This awareness of keeping *thuenlam*, coupled with the giving nature of the Bhutanese, makes them extremely hospitable and always ready to lend a helping hand. Thus the simple act of sharing and giving is deeply engrained in the culture. Families support each other; friends, colleagues, and neighbors go out of their way unhesitatingly to lend assistance when needed; and in villages the traditions of community participation are visible. Bhutan's rugged mountains and harsh living conditions, coupled with its small population, have greatly inclined the people and the society to rely on each other. This can also be strongly attributed to the Buddhist practice of *jimba*, meaning selfless acts of charity to the poor and needy without any expectations of return. It is often the lay people who support the monks with basic material necessities.

A distinctive form of sharing and giving still in practice in the villages is that of *woola*—the contribution of labor made by every household to help build a house for a family or to undertake larger constructions such as monasteries, schools, and hospitals in the community. To see and hear an entire village singing and working together to build a house is a heartening experience.

With modern education, there is a growing civil society sector where educated Bhutanese contribute time and resources for a common cause. There are organizations dedicated to common issues of youth unemployment, raising awareness about health and education, and tackling social issues such as drug use.

RELIGION, CUSTOMS, & TRADITIONS

Bhutan is the only Buddhist country in the world where the Tantric form of Mahayana Buddhism (known in the West as Vajrayana Buddhism, or the "Diamond Vehicle") is the main religion. The constitution of Bhutan upholds Buddhism as the "spiritual heritage" of the country and the king as the protector of all religions. Buddhism plays a pivotal role in everyday life. The prayer flags dotting the countryside, numerous monasteries and temples, paintings on walls, and carvings on hillsides are all constant reminders of the deep influence of Buddhist beliefs and aspirations. The prevailing culture not only draws inspiration from the past but also remains deeply rooted in long-established traditions.

While Mahayana Buddhism in its Tantric form is the dominant religion in the country, with over 75 percent of the population (mainly the Drukpa) following it, Hinduism is widely practiced among the Lhotshampa of the south, descendants of Nepali immigrants, who make up nearly 25 percent of the population. In recent years there has been a small number of Christian converts as well.

Bon—a pre-Buddhist, shamanic religion that worshiped all forms of nature and spirits—was once widely practiced; some of its practices have been incorporated into the mainstream of Tantric Buddhism, and are particularly evident in the various Bhutanese rituals and popular beliefs.

The schools or sects of Buddhism that exist today in Bhutan are the official Drukpa Kagyu, a branch of the Kagyupa sect, and the Nyingmapa, the oldest school. The latter is more widely followed in central and eastern Bhutan.

BUDDHISM

Different Schools of Buddhism in Bhutan
Buddhism evolved from the teachings of Siddhartha Gautama, a royal prince of the Shakya clan, who lived in northern India in the sixth century BCE. When Gautama discovered the human pain and suffering endured in sickness and in old age, he renounced all worldly pleasures and embarked on a spiritual quest for the solution to the problem of suffering. After six years of extreme asceticism, he reverted to the "Middle Way" of meditation, and, sitting beneath a tree, concentrated on seeing things as they are. Passing through four layers of progressive insight, he reached enlightenment.

Young monks on their way to Phajoding Monastery near Thimphu.

The Buddha recognized "Four Noble Truths": namely, that suffering exists, that suffering has a cause, that suffering can end, and that there is a path to the ending of suffering. The Noble Eightfold Path is the essence of the Middle Way, the path between the extremes of self-indulgence and denial. These were Right Speech, Right Action, Right Livelihood, Right Effort, Right Mindfulness, Right Concentration, Right View, and Right Intention.

After the Buddha's death, differences arose among his disciples and, over time, different schools of thought appeared, bringing in their own interpretation of the teachings. The two principal sects in the beginning were the Hinayana and the Mahayana. Hinayana, also known as Theravada, largely practiced in Southeast Asia, focuses mainly on pursuing liberation for the individual. Mahayana, on the other hand, lays emphasis on compassion for and liberation of all sentient beings as well as oneself. This altruistic attitude is referred to as *bodhicitta* or *jang chub sem*, "the desire to realize enlightenment for the sake of others." Further, under Mahayana, different schools emerged, each derived from a distinctive lineage. The oldest is Nyingmapa, which traces its origin back to the great Indian saint Guru Padmasambhava, who came to Tibet in the eighth century CE. Between the ninth and twelfth centuries, Mahayana Buddhism saw the emergence of three major schools of Tantric Buddhism in Tibet—the Kagyupa, the Kadampa, and the Sagyapa. The fourth, Gelugpa, originated in the fourteenth century. Its current spiritual head is the Dalai Lama.

The Arrival of Buddhism in Bhutan

Buddhism was first introduced to Bhutan in the seventh century CE, when the powerful Tibetan king, Songtsen Gampo, constructed the first two Buddhist temples—Kyichhu Lhakhang in Paro and Jambay Lhakhang in Bumthang. About half a century later, the Indian Buddhist saint Padmasambhava, popularly referred to as Guru Rinpoche, "The Precious Jewel," arrived in Bhutan at the invitation of Sindhu Raja, ruler in the region of Bumthang in central Bhutan.

After successfully subjugating the demons and deities and converting the king as well, Padmasambhava left for Tibet. On his second visit, he resided in Bumthang, and during his stay built many monasteries across Bhutan. He is regarded as the founder of the

Nyingmapa school, the oldest religious sect, and is often referred to as the "Second Buddha."

With the visit of Guru Padmasambhava, Buddhism began to put down firm roots in Bhutan. In the following centuries, many Buddhist masters and scholars arrived from Tibet—some fleeing persecution—and settled in the valleys of central and eastern Bhutan, bringing with them a rich collection of Buddhist scriptures and establishing monasteries. Finally, it was the arrival of Zhabdrung Ngawang Namgyal from Tibet in 1616 that cemented Drukpa Kagyu as Bhutan's state religion within the overall framework of the dual system of governance that continues until this day.

Mahayana Buddhism: the Tantric Form

Tantric Buddhism emerged in India in about the sixth century CE, and while it has long disappeared from its country of origin, this form of Buddhism spread farther north, and over the next several centuries across the Himalayas to Bhutan, Tibet, Nepal, China, Mongolia, and Japan, and to parts of India, such as Ladakh in Jammu and Kashmir, and Sikkim.

The word *tantra* refers to a collection of esoteric texts supposed to have been left behind in secret by Sakyamuni (that is, the Wise One, or Sage of the Sakya clan) Buddha to a select few of his disciples. Tantric Buddhism is no different from other forms of Buddhism. It follows the same fundamental beliefs— that there is consequence to your actions (*karma*) and this results in reincarnation. Tantric Buddhism calls for the collective attainment of *nirvana* (meaning the "blowing out" of entanglement or attachment), freedom from all suffering, the ultimate spiritual goal for Buddhists. This is achieved through rigorous practice involving mystical forces, various rituals, and the recitation of *mantras* (words chanted repetitively as aids to meditation). The popular *mantras* are *Om Mani Padma Hung* to Chenresig—the Compassionate One—and *Om Ah Hung Vajra Guru Padma Siddhi Hung*—the eight-word *mantra* to Padmasambhava (Guru Rinpoche). An important aspect of Tantric Buddhism is the pantheon of symbolic deities and *Bodhisattvas*, which translates as "Buddhas to be." They are enlightened beings who have attained *nirvana* but have chosen to be reborn on Earth and live among the humans to help them alleviate suffering.

It is important to note that, as Tantric Buddhism evolved, it began to assimilate certain elements or practices of pre-Buddhist, shamanic religion such as nature worship and animal sacrifice. The *nep* is the local deity of a particular area: for example, the *yulha* are the guardian deities whose abodes are in the mountain peaks, and the *tsho-men* is the spirit that dwells in the lake.

The colorful paintings and murals on the walls of the monasteries and temples depict Tantric teachings. Some images appear terrifying and even demonic, with blazing eyes, and numerous heads and hands. However, beneath the pageantry lies a profound meaning. They are merely emanations from peaceful deities that assume wrathful forms to subdue evil spirits hostile to Buddhism. Some of the figures are depicted in sexual union with their female counterparts. In Tantric Buddhism, the male and female figures in unison represent the primordial union of wisdom and compassion. Tara is the most important female deity, the savior *Bodhisattva* whose mantra, "*Om tare tutare ture svaha*," is very popular. She is known as the "mother of liberation," and embodies universal compassion that supersedes even the "love of a mother for her child."

Performing rituals is a big part of Tantric Buddhism. There are different rituals for specific purposes—to invoke rain or banish illnesses, or to overcome hostile forces and bring prosperity. Ritual objects such as the *dorje* (thunderbolt), the *phurpa* (dagger), and the *drilbui* (bell) are some of the main objects used during religious ceremonies, along with offerings of *tormas*, which are decorated cakes made of butter and flour.

The Drukpa Kagyu

The great religious master Tsangpa Gyare Yeshe Dorje founded the Drukpa Kagyu school at the Ralung monastery in Tibet in the twelfth century. Legend has it that, on his deathbed, Tsangpa Gyare prophesied that a young man from eastern Tibet would come and, upon receiving all of the Drukpa teachings, would travel south and spread the teachings in western Bhutan. This young man was Phajo Drugom Shigpo, who, in 1222, traveled to western Bhutan and introduced the Drukpa lineage as prophesied. At the turn of the century, another Buddhist master, Gyalwa Lorepa, visited Bumthang in central Bhutan and founded the Chodrak monastery. Following him, many eminent Buddhist masters soon visited Bhutan, but it was not until the arrival of Zhabdrung Ngawang Namgyal (see pages 30) that Drukpa Kagyu firmly established itself as the main Buddhist sect in Bhutan.

The Kagyu lineage practices the important points of both *sutra* (collections of the discourses of Buddha) and *tantra* (esoteric teachings on macro–microcosmic correspondence, couched as a dialog), with emphasis on the Tantric teachings of the Vajrayana (the "Diamond Vehicle"). Vajrayana uses specific practices and Mahamudra (Great Seal) teachings for the attainment of enlightenment in a single lifetime. It also emphasizes the continuity of teachings and oral instructions passed on from master to student. The great Indian masters Tilopa, Naropa, and Maitripa, and later the great Tibetan master yogis Marpa, his disciple Milarepa, and Milarepa's disciple Gampopa are some of those who contributed hundreds of volumes of teachings that preserve the lineage.

Lama Drukpa Kuenley

Of the numerous saints and scholars who visited Bhutan in the course of the centuries, the Tibetan lama Drukpa Kuenley (1455–1529) is without doubt the most popular Buddhist master in Bhutanese history. He is mostly remembered for his unconventional and at times outrageous methods of teaching—usually with strong sexual overtones and bawdy humor. Fascinating tales abound about the eccentric saint who was known for his drinking habits and womanizing, and his complete disregard for social norms. His wayward ways earned him the name "Divine Madman."

But his untamed habits are said to be guises under which the saint realized his teachings. It is said that he subdued demons with a wooden phallus, hitting them on the head with it. The wooden phallus is now the symbolic representation of fertility. With his unusual but very giving nature, Lama Drukpa Kuenley came to be known for his all-wish-fulfilling power—giving life and liberation to people, and defying conventional law and morality.

Chimi Lhakhang Monastery in Lobesa was built after he subdued a cannibal demoness with his "thunderbolt wisdom," and you will find numerous wooden phalluses in the monastery. People from all over the country and abroad come to seek his blessings, especially couples who wish for children. Phallus paintings on walls of the houses are a common sight, particularly in western Bhutan. The colorful, embellished images are said to ward off evil spirits.

The Nyingmapa

The Nyingmapa lineage is the oldest of the major schools of Tibetan Buddhism. As we have seen, it traces its origin to the Indian master Guru Padmasambhava, who, at the invitation of the Tibetan King Trisong Deutsen (742–97), traveled to Tibet to help him establish Buddhism there. Another Indian Buddhist master, Shantarakshita, was already in Tibet to help the king in this, but as they were facing numerous obstacles from the local deities and spirits, Shantarakshita advised the king to invite Guru Padmasambhava to subdue them. Through his compassion and wisdom, Guru Padmasambhava pacified the spirits and made them Dharma protectors; and so Buddhism was successfully established in Tibet.

Guru Padmasambhava transmitted Vajrayana teachings to his first twenty-five disciples, who all became renowned Buddhist masters with great spiritual accomplishments. The tradition even survived vicious persecution by King Langdarma in the ninth century.

In the early years the Nyingmapa lineage was not based on institutional structures. Rather it focused on individual oral transmission, continuous and unbroken from master to student. The lineage became more institutionalized later, and by the fifteenth century many great monasteries had been established in Tibet.

An important aspect of the Nyingmapa lineage is the *terma* tradition. As we have seen, *terma* are a class of texts that were concealed on their creation with the intention that they should be discovered at a later date. It is believed that Guru Padmasambhava hid hundreds of scriptures, images, and ritual articles throughout Tibet and the Himalayas with specific instructions on how to discover and reveal these "treasures," as they came to be known, for the benefit of future generations. The discoverer was known as a *terton*, or "treasure revealer." These lineages of revealed teachings include the Dzogchen tradition, or the "Great Completion."

Death

Death in Buddhism emphasizes awareness of impermanence. Everything is momentary and constantly changing, and death is an unavoidable stage of every life on this Earth. Buddhists place much significance on death. It does not mean the end but merely the passing into another life. Soon after a person has died, monks, or *gomchens*, are called to perform complex rituals necessary for the guidance of the dead. *Phowa,* the meditation practice for guiding the consciousness at the moment before death, is an important ritual performed by a high lama, a master monk. The mark of a successful *phowa* is a small drop of blood directly from the center of the crown of the head. Specific prayers and rituals last up to forty-nine days, if possible without interruption. The cremation day and time are decided by an astrologer, based on the name, age, and time of death of the deceased. After the cremation the ashes are scattered in a river. Sometimes the bones are collected, ground, and mixed with clay to make *tsa tsas* (votive offerings shaped in a mold). Prayer flags are hoisted and *chortens* (shrines) are built to bring merit to the deceased. Every year on the anniversary of the death the deceased is remembered; elaborate ceremonies are held in the house, and offerings are made in monasteries.

Rebirth

In Buddhism life does not end with death but is one in an endless and countless succession of lives. All sentient beings are trapped in *samsara*, the cycle of rebirth. In Mahayana Buddhism it is believed that the deceased will be reborn in one of six realms within forty-nine days and will no longer be wandering in *bardo*, the intermediate state between death and rebirth.

According to Buddhist doctrine, rebirth can happen in any of the six realms of existence depicted on the Wheel of Rebirth, also known as the Wheel of Life. These six realms include the three good realms of gods, demigods, and human beings, and the three lower realms of animals, hungry ghosts, and hell. The realms are also understood as psychological as much as physical states. In Mahayana Buddhism it is regarded as extremely fortunate to be reborn as a human being, which allows one a good chance to pursue the spiritual path to attain Buddhahood, or *nirvana*, the ending of the vicious cycle of death and rebirth, the ultimate goal of Buddhists.

Karma: The Law of Cause and Effect

The word *karma* is Sanskrit for "action," or "deed." All actions have consequences, and whether an action is good or bad depends on the underlying intention. These actions can be not only physical but also speech and thought. The Buddha taught that one's present life is only one in a beginning-less series of incarnations, and each of these is determined by one's actions in previous lives: "What you are is what you have been, what you will be is what you do now." However, not all consequences of one's actions are immediate. They may come to fruition now, at different stages of life, or in the next life, or in a future life. The concept of *karma* is not based on ideas of justice or punishment (fear of the consequences of disobedience), or pre-planned by the Almighty. Buddhists believe in personal responsibility for shaping one's own destiny by the accruing of merit. For the Bhutanese, *karma* and the associated principles of *ley-jumdrey* and interdependence (see page 53) are their guides to everyday activities.

The Monastic Community and Monkhood

Although Buddhism arrived in Bhutan in the seventh century CE, it was only in the seventeenth century that the Zhung Dratsang, the formal monastic community that is the state clergy responsible for all religious affairs, was established by Zhabdrung Ngawang Namgyal. The first monastic center was set up in Cheri, about eight and a half miles (14 km) from the capital Thimphu, around 1621 with a group of thirty monks. The Zhabdrung went on to create a strong Drukpa state and renamed the country "Druk" and the people "Drukpa" to indicate the supremacy of the Drukpa lineage. Religion and secular administration were given equal importance. As we have seen, Zhabdrung introduced the role of Je Khenpo, or Chief Abbot, as the spiritual leader and head of the monastic community in the country, while all temporal matters were assigned to an appointed regent known as the Druk Desi. The tradition continues to the present day, and the king now appoints the Je Khenpo on the recommendation of five eminent monks from the Dratsang Lhengtsog (Commission of Monastic

Monks at the entrance to Tashichho Monestary in Thimphu.

Affairs). The *rabde*, or the district monastic community, is headed by the Lam Neten and the community resides in the *dzong*. The *dzong* also houses the district government offices.

The Zhung Dratsang continues to play an important role in the spiritual and cultural lives of the Bhutanese. Today there are more than seven thousand ordained monks (*gelong*), largely of the Drukpa clergy, residing in different centers and monasteries throughout the country. Ordained monks wear the characteristic maroon robe and shave their heads. Boys are usually sent at a young age to join the monastery, or *goemba*—a gesture that confers great prestige on the family. It is also likely that these boys will come from poorer backgrounds and have little or no say in the decision.

These monasteries are called *lobdra*, and are equivalent to primary education, where the young monks are taught Buddhist philosophy, poetry, and grammar, learn to memorize prayers, and train in Buddhist art forms and rituals with the use of different religious instruments. University-level higher learning is called *shedra* and involves many more years of rigorous learning, training, and practice.

They progress through various stages of vows before becoming fully ordained monks. Once ordained, they abstain from smoking and drinking and are celibate. If anyone decides to leave, he can do so on paying a fine to the monastic body. Those who drop out are called

Young monks in personal study.

getey, or "retired monks," and there is no social stigma for having done so.

Though the state looks after the monastic centers and takes care of their basic needs, the monks also visit people's homes in order to perform religious ceremonies for events such as birth, marriage, illness, or death, and are offered cash for their services, which they can keep. There are also monks of the Nyingmapa School, who are mainly supported by private patronage. A large number of these are *gomchens*, or lay monks. Unlike the ordained monks who live in the monastery and are celibate, *gomchens* have families and live at home. They are important part of the community, as they perform all the religious ceremonies in the villages and homes, especially in places where monks are not easily available.

In comparison, there are fewer nuns practicing in Bhutan and few monasteries dedicated to them. Not all monasteries have monks in residence or provide monastic education. A small village monastery or one located in a remote place will have a caretaker, or *kaynur*, to look after the complex. The bigger monasteries with monastic schools are either under the Zhung Dratsang or in the care of *trulkus* or *rinpoches* (see below*)*. Some monasteries are also privately owned. Another common Buddhist structure is the *chorten*, often found built high on a mountain pass or down by the confluence of a river. These conical structures contain relics and idols of Buddhist deities, and the architectural design is symbolic and meaningful.

Trulku

A *trulku*, which literally translates as "transformation body," is the reincarnation of a great master. The lineage can be centuries long, with a succession of reincarnations. This was seen as an important means for assuring not only the spiritual but also the political continuity of the monastic institutions and lineages. Once recognized, a *trulku* undergoes rigorous monastic training and assumes the spiritual duties from his previous life. The highly regarded *trulkus* are called *Rinpoche*, "Great Precious One," and many conduct important blessing ceremonies and impart teachings to the public. The *trulku* system does not exist in other branches of Buddhism such as Hinayana or Zen.

Tshechu: The Buddhist Festival

Tshechus are religious festivals held annually in temples, monasteries, and *dzongs* throughout the country. *Tshechu* literally translates as the "tenth day," and is celebrated in honor of Guru Rinpoche, who was born on the tenth day of the sixth Bhutanese lunar month. The official annual *tshechu* for each district is held at the *dzong*. Other monasteries hold their own annual *tshechus* at different times of the year. A *tshechu* is celebrated for several days, mostly for three to five days, and usually ends with the unfurling of a giant *thangkha* (scroll painting) called a *thongdrol*; the Bhutanese stand in line to receive blessings. Monks offer prayers, and colorful and varied mask dances are performed outside in the courtyards by monks, *gomchens*, and lay people.

The Bhutanese consider it important to attend *tshechus*, as they believe that witnessing the mask dances and being part of the festival will create and accumulate merit and blessings. Besides their religious significance, *tshechus* are also a time for social gathering, when people from all walks of life put on their best clothes, take a break from work, and relax with their family and friends. *Tshechus* are also a big

Monks playing *lingm* flutes as part of the festivities.

A woman perfroms at the Thimphu *teschu* celebrations.

attraction for tourists, who plan their holidays around
the popular ones such as the Paro Tshechu in spring
and the Thimphu Tshechu in fall.

Food Offerings

Food has a special role to play in religious ceremonies
throughout Bhutan. It is offered at important religious
rituals called *rimdoe* or *choego*. These are performed
on all occasions—births, marriages, deaths, official
functions, annual household ceremonies, illness, and
when sitting exams, to name a few. The offerings are
laid at altars and shrines to obtain what one wishes for.
At a *tshechu*, mountains of food—anything edible—are
generously offered during the ceremonies and later
distributed to the people, who receive it as a blessing.
People will also bring food to offer when making
monastery visits. The practice is considered to bestow
blessings and bring about favorable situations.

Spectators flock to Tashichho Dzong to watch the mask dances of the Thimphu *teschu*.

Mask Dances

Mask dances, called *cham*, are specially performed during a *tshechu*, depicting and describing, through movement and music, the teachings of Buddha and the *dharma*. They are broadly categorized into three distinct themes: dances with moral stories; dances that purify and protect from destructive spirits; and dances that celebrate the triumph of Buddhism and glorify Guru Rinpoche and his deeds.

The dances are a powerful way of bringing Buddhism closer to the people, who largely depend on the clergy for guidance on the spiritual path. The Bhutanese believe that the mere act of watching the *cham* allows the spectators to gain merit and receive a special blessing.

Dancers at Punakha Dzong.

Atsaras (clowns) are an interesting feature of the festival ground, frolicking around and entertaining the crowd with their antics, and often brandish a large wooden phallus.

Each dance is meaningful, but some, with their dramatic narratives and visual splendor, are particularly popular with the audience. The *Raksha Marcham*, or the Dance of the Judgment of the Dead, is one of the most interesting mask dances performed at the *tshechus*. The drama unfolds with the dance of the *Rakshas*, the aides of the God of Death, Shinje Choekyi Gyalpo. It is Judgement Day, and the first to appear before the God of Death is a sinner, dressed all in black. His sins outweigh his good actions, and he is sent to hell. Then comes another person, dressed in white, and again, the God hears his deeds. He is found to be virtuous and led to the pure land.

The *Shanag*, or the Black Hat Dance, is spectacular. Monks dressed in silky brocade robes and with wide, fur-trimmed hats perched on their heads gracefully twirl and jump around the courtyard to the rhythmic beatings of the drum. The dance symbolizes the exorcising of the demonic forces from the dancing area. It also depicts the epic story of the killing of anti-Buddhist Tibetan king Langdharma in the ninth century by a Buddhist monk, thus purifying and protecting the Buddhist *dharma*.

The *Guru Tshengye*, or the Dance of the Eight Manifestations of Guru Rinpoche, is usually performed on the last day. It is a dramatic display involving eight solo dances, each commemorating a specific episode in the life of Guru Rinpoche.

HINDUISM

Hinduism is the other major religion in Bhutan. It is commonly practiced among the Lhotshampa community of the south, who make up roughly 25 percent of the population. Hinduism is the world's oldest religion and, unlike other world religions, it has no human founder. Originally an oral tradition believed to have been divinely revealed to visionaries, the earliest Hindu teachings are found in the scriptures known as the *Vedas* (written between 1500 and 900 BCE).

Monks perform *Shanag,* the Black Hat Dance.

These contain the core principles, beliefs, practices, and philosophy of Hinduism. Hymns and prayers from the Vedic texts are chanted during ceremonies and prayers to invoke the gods. One major feature of the Vedic period is the Hindu caste system: *Brahmins* (priests, or *Bahuns* in the Lhotshampa language, Nepali), *Chhetris* (warriors), *Vaisyas* (traders and farmers), and *Sudras* (menial workers). Despite the many gods worshiped, Hindus believe in a Supreme Being—Brahman, or the Supreme Self. He is the creator, preserver, revealer, and destroyer, who pervades and envelops the whole of creation and resides in all. The Hindu deities and their consorts are manifestations of Brahman.

In 2015, Shivalaya Mandir, the first *mandir* (Hindu temple) dedicated to Lord Shiva, was constructed in the southern town of Samtse. A large temple for the goddess Durga, Devi Panchayan Mandir, was completed in Thimphu in 2019. Every year, the king celebrates the Hindu festival of Dashain with the people, sharing in the festivity and fun. It is also not uncommon for Bhutanese Hindus to visit Buddhist monasteries and offer prayers and to attend Buddhist prayer festivals and *tshechus*.

THE BHUTANESE CALENDAR

The Bhutanese lunar calendar is a variant form of the Tibetan calendar, which in turn is influenced by the Indian and Chinese calendars. It is calculated by a complex set of rules. The Bhutanese year begins in February and, is divided into twelve months. Each year is also assigned to a particular animal and element. With twelve animals, there is a natural twelve-year cycle, which completes a *lho khor*. The older generation still use *lho khor* to refer to and calculate years. For instance, if you are thirty-six years old, you would have completed *lho khor sum* (three). Particular days in a month are also given significance and classified as auspicious or inauspicious according to the position of the celestial bodies. People refrain from making journeys on the second, eighth, fourteenth, twentieth, and twenty-sixth days of the month, as it is *ta shi ga chhag* (broken saddle, dead horse) and considered inauspicious for travel. Sometimes a whole year is also deemed inauspicious—a *lho-na* (black year)—as the year 2016 was. A surge of construction projects were reported toward the end of 2015 as people hurried to start building before the *lho-na* year began.

THE FESTIVE YEAR

The Bhutanese love of pageantry, pomp, and ceremony is evident in their many unique, colorful, and often spectacular festivals.

January, February, March
Chunipa Losar
The "Traditional Day of Offering" is celebrated on the first day of the twelfth month of the Bhutanese calendar, and is devoted to making offerings of thanksgiving and ritual feasting. Historically it was on this day that people gathered from all over the country to make offerings to the Zhabdrung at the Punakha Dzong as an expression of their love, devotion, and loyalty.

Dangpai Losar
This is the New Year in Bhutan—as it is also in Tibet—and is observed throughout the country, either with early-morning prayers in the family shrine room, or with a visit to the monastery to pray

and make offerings for a prosperous year. People usually refrain from doing anything negative on this day, to ensure a smooth and uneventful year ahead.

February 21: The King's Birthday
This is a three-day holiday, beginning on February 21. Various cultural events are held in schools and districts.

May, June, July
Zhabdrung Kuchoe
On the tenth day of the third Bhutanese month, he country marks the anniversary of the death of Zhabdrung Ngawang Namgyal, the Unifier of Bhutan. On this day in 1651 he is believed to have "entered into a retreat" and remained in this state for many years. The day is now observed as the anniversary of his death. Offices and schools are closed for the day, and people visit monasteries to offer prayers and butter lamps to mark the anniversary.

Lord Buddha's Parinirvana, or Duechen Nga Zom
This is observed on the fifteenth day of the fourth month of the Bhutanese calendar. It was on this day that Buddha was conceived, was born, subdued evil, gained enlightenment, and left this life, attaining nirvana. It is considered to be one of the most auspicious days not only for the Bhutanese but for Buddhists all over the world. Special prayers are held in all the important monasteries, and in Thimphu

devotees throng the Trashichho Dzong to receive blessings from the huge *thongdrol* that is unfurled.

The Birth Anniversary of Guru Padmasambhava

Another important public holiday is the Birth Anniversary of Guru Padmasambhava, or Guru Rinpoche, as he is popularly known in Bhutan. It is celebrated on the tenth day of the fifth month of the Bhutanese calendar, which typically falls in June or July in the Gregorian calendar. Prayers are conducted in monasteries throughout the country, and the Bhutanese devote the day to prayer and gaining merit.

Drukpa Tshe Zhi, the First Sermon of Lord Buddha

This is observed every fourth day of the sixth month in the Bhutanese calendar, and it is considered the most significant and auspicious day in the Buddhist calendar. It was on this day that Buddha Shakyamuni gave his first sermon in the Deer Park at Sarnath, in India, after attaining enlightenment. He taught the Middle Way: refraining from extremes of pleasure; the practice of austerity; the following of the Four Noble Truths, and the Eightfold Paths, which became known as the First Turning of the Wheel of Dharma.

September, October
Thrue Bab

This day, the "Blessed Rainy Day," marks the end of the monsoon season in Bhutan. During the auspicious hour, all waters on Earth are believed to be sanctifying, and people are encouraged to take an outdoor bath to

Culture Smart! **Bhutan**

be cleansed of "bad deeds, defilement, and accumulated bad *karma*." The most favorable hour for the ablution ceremony is determined by astrologers from the Zhung Dratsang, the central monastic body.

Dasain
Dasain is an important festival for Hindus celebrating the victory of the goddess Durga over the demon Mahishasura. The festivities last for several days, with significant events taking place every day until the tenth day, when families get together to celebrate and enjoy enormous meals. Parents put *tikka* (made of rice, yogurt, and vermilion) on the children's foreheads for a happy and prosperous life.

November/December
Lhabab Duechen
This falls on the twenty-second day of the ninth Bhutanese month. It marks the day on which Buddha returned to Earth from the realm of the gods, after giving teachings to his mother, who was reborn there. Special prayers are held in monasteries and people offer their prayers at home, visit monasteries, offer butter lamps, and give alms to the poor or needy. It is believed that all positive or negative actions on this day are multiplied ten million times.

Ngenpa Guzom
This day, the "Meeting of Nine Evils," has recently been removed from the national holiday list, but nonetheless it is one of the popular festive events still

observed. The day falls on the seventh day of the eleventh Bhutanese month. People refrain from doing any important work, in the belief that nothing good can be achieved on this day. In eastern Bhutan the day is a festive occasion on which to eat, drink, and make merry.

Nyilo

This translates as "A Good Year," and coincides with the winter solstice. It is mainly celebrated as New Year in the western region of Bhutan. Groups of young children visit homes and sing *lolay* (songs like carols). They are usually grouped in odd numbers, because even numbers are considered to bring bad luck.

CHAPTER FOUR

MAKING FRIENDS

The Bhutanese often joke that, "Everyone knows everyone in Bhutan." As a small country with a tiny population, no one is a complete stranger. There would always be a common friend or acquaintance, and this helps to make connections quickly and develop friendships. Knowing the right people and having a good network of people is important in Bhutan, particularly if you want to get things done quickly. In a small society, relationships are easily built through your school or your family, and often in face-to-face settings rather than by written means.

The close-knit society often means that people will favor those they know, especially in service areas such as hospitals, utility companies, and banks. This is especially true in cases where the bureaucracy makes things slow for ordinary people.

While social gatherings are largely among family and extended family, the Bhutanese do like to spend time with friends. But it's not all about having fun together.

People respect and value their friends and expect to take care of and support each other in times of need. A person's circle of friends usually consists of cousins of the same age group, childhood friends, and school and college friends, who go on to be lifelong friends. Although social background is not a key factor in determining who you are friends with, people do tend to move around with those who have things in common, such as archery or football after school or work.

MEETING PEOPLE

Socializing in Bhutan takes place mainly at home. In the rural areas the entire village comes together to help at religious ceremonies conducted at home and during festivals, to share work, and to take part in the celebrations.

In the urban centers, Western-style cafés, bars, and restaurants are popular places for friends to meet up. Numerous snooker and videogame parlors that have opened up in the town centers in recent years are popular venues for young people to hang out. It is common to see people, especially the elderly, gathering at the monasteries and stupas, either circumambulating or sitting around in groups with prayer beads and prayer wheels in hand.

Communication with the majority of the people in the urban centers will not be a problem, as English is widely spoken among the educated. Visitors will find that the Bhutanese can initially be quite reserved and

that they may take a while to thaw. However, once you get to know them, you will find them to be genuinely warm and sincere.

GREETINGS AND OTHER COURTESIES

Greetings in Bhutan depend on the person you are meeting. On meeting someone for the first time in an informal setting, you bow slightly and with a nod of the head, say "*Kuzuzangpo*," (literally, "May you be blessed with good health"). It is also usual to extend both hands in a closed handshake.

In a formal greeting to a superior or an important person, you take a short step forward and make a low bow, with both hands in front and palms shown. Keep your head slightly bowed and your gaze on the ground as a mark of respect.

Important religious heads or Buddhist masters are greeted with three prostrations, as you would do in a monastery. A suffix, *la*, is added as a mark of respect, as in "*Kuzuzangpo-la!*" When a superior enters the room, everyone is expected to stand up until asked to sit. While taking leave, it is important that you do not abruptly turn your back. Taking a few backward steps and making a slight bow is the respectful way to leave.

WHAT'S IN A NAME?

In Bhutan, especially among the Drukpa, personal names do not include family names or surnames, with the exception of the royal family. After a child is born two names are given by a monk, usually with some meaning or religious connotation. Most names are common; for example, during your visit you may come across many people named Karma Choden. To complicate things further, most names can be given to both boys and girls. However, there are a few exceptions; names such as Choden, Wangmo, Deki, and Dema are typically feminine, while Wangdi, Tobgye, Chedup, and Gyeltshen are names for men.

After marriage a woman retains her own name, and the children do not carry their father's name, as happens in the West or other South Asian countries. However, as more Bhutanese travel abroad with their families and have reportedly faced difficulties at immigration with different names, children are now given the second name of their father as their "family name," in addition to their own two names.

In southern Bhutan, a predominantly Hindu society, family surnames are given, which are mostly based on the person's caste or tribe.

SOCIALIZING WITH WORK COLLEAGUES

Although socializing with work colleagues may not involve the after-work drinking culture as in the West, it is an important part of office life in Bhutan, where, over time, those working together develop close bonds and friendship. The relaxed, friendly nature of the Bhutanese makes it easier for someone to join a new office, where they will be made welcome. Colleagues are referred to as "office friends," and they lunch together, talk about their families, and even discuss personal matters with one another, extending or receiving advice in times of need. The men, especially those who are single, often get together for a game of football or an archery session after office hours or on weekends.

There is also a culture of sharing moments that goes beyond the office walls. In the event of a death in the family or the arrival of a newborn, colleagues come together and pay a visit to the family, bearing gifts, or they extend monetary and moral support.

Given the hierarchical culture, a senior colleague or a boss is referred to as *Dasho* or *Aum* (equivalent to Sir or Madam), and never called by his or her first name. You may do things together, but the protocol is always maintained. Using first names among similar age groups is common, however.

As in any other cultural setting, senior colleagues of either sex always command respect, and a certain decorum is observed. Among coworkers, there are no specific norms to follow when it comes to socializing with the opposite sex, and women and men hang out and talk to each other as regular friends.

INVITATIONS HOME

The Bhutanese are hospitable, warm, and friendly people, always ready with a smile. It is not uncommon to be invited to their homes and offered tea or even a good meal. There is no concept of making plans or appointments when calling on someone. Guests are treated generously and served the best food and drinks the host can offer. A special guest is served a full meal with a variety of dishes at any time of day. If you plan to visit a couple of homes on the same day, you will have to be prepared to eat more than just three meals that day! Guests are seated in the main room, which is often the shrine room, and given the best seat while the host might stand or sit on a chair or on the floor next to the door. Sometimes, if visiting a humble family in the village, the hosts disappear and leave the guests alone in the family room. They will reappear only to serve drinks and food but will not eat along with the guests.

MANNERS

Table manners are important. Dining etiquette is strictly adhered to as required by *driglam-namzha*, where one must not make slurping noises, chomp food loudly, or eat before everyone else has been served. The Bhutanese eat with their right hand. Rice is made into small balls and dipped in the stew served in bowls. When tea is offered, guests hold the cup or bowl in both hands while being served. When drinking tea with a superior, one should hold the cup and not place it on the table. It is polite to take a few sips and accept a second serving (*droen*) when offered. In eastern Bhutan, *chang* or *ara*, home-brewed alcohol, is served instead.

Leaving food on the plate is not considered polite, and throwing away food is not accepted. Guests are always served first and hosts will wait until their guests start eating before serving themselves.

It is polite to bring along a simple gift for your host. Visiting a

A woman serves ara, home-brewed alcohol, to her guests.

farmhouse and enjoying a typical meal with the host family has become a popular activity for tourists during their visits.

SOCIALIZING WITH THE OPPOSITE SEX

Men and women can spend time together in ordinary friendships, sharing jokes and enjoying an easy camaraderie. Physical gestures like touching a hand or a shoulder, or giving a friendly hug, are all acceptable, as long as these don't cross the barrier between friendship and sexual advance.

Dating is common among teens and young adults, especially in urban centers, though you may not see public displays of affection as commonly as you do in the West. While messaging apps like WhatsApp and WeChat play an increasing role when it comes to socializing, dating apps largely do not, though this may start to change over time. Bhutanese society may have a liberal attitude toward sex and relationships, but it is definitely not promiscuous.

MEETING WITH OUTSIDERS

When Bhutan opened its doors to welcome the outside world in the early 1970s, only a handful of foreign diplomats, volunteers, friends of the elite, and tourists came to visit the country. The visitors were mainly confined to Thimphu, except for teaching and health volunteers, who were placed in remote villages across the country. There are accounts of curious villagers, unaccustomed to seeing those who come from faraway lands, turning up at the door "to have a look at the *chilip*." This term for a Westerner is at once affectionate but slightly disparaging.

As elsewhere, the Bhutanese are fascinated with all things foreign. They are genuinely interested to know you, and want to find out about other cultures. But at the same time, they will not speak to you unless spoken to, out of respect. A visitor once remarked that "in Bhutan, you are not followed around with stares or hounded for a picture," which is often the case with being a tourist in a foreign land. The urban, educated Bhutanese will happily engage in conversation with you, and will welcome discussions and different points of view on various topics. Striking up a direct conversation with those who have not been to school can be challenging because of the language barrier, but you will have impromptu translators in young schoolchildren, eager to hear your story and share their own.

There is a small but well-connected expat community in Bhutan, based in Thimphu, largely made up of staff from different UN organizations and several bilateral and multilateral development agencies from European countries such as Sweden, Switzerland, the Netherlands, Denmark, and Austria. There are currently no Western consulates in Bhutan, though there are a few from neighbouring countries.

CHAPTER FIVE

AT HOME

HOUSING

Traditional Bhutanese houses bear remarkable similarities to Buddhist monasteries and *dzongs* in architecture and design. The solid walls, shingled sloping roof, and carved window frames richly decorated with paintings are strikingly beautiful, and unique to Bhutan. In rural areas the materials used are largely stone, wood, and rammed earth, whereas houses in the urban areas are modern, built with a mixture of bricks, stone, sand, and cement. Modern buildings must follow strict building regulations and incorporate traditional architectural features, which lend a degree of uniformity, beautifully merging the old with the new. Some argue that the result is more like "a row of matchboxes," devoid of character and individualism. All houses must be roofed, and buildings in Thimphu and other urban towns are restricted to five stories, with roofs painted either maroon or green for aesthetic appeal.

Traditional rural housing.

In some parts of eastern Bhutan and in the low-lying plains of the south, bamboo is widely used to build houses that stand on stilts to avoid being flooded during the monsoon. The semi-nomadic yak herders of the far north usually live in dry-stone-walled houses or tents made of yak hair.

The traditional houses in the rural areas are two to three stories high. The ground floor serves as a storeroom and a shelter for the animals. The family occupies the next floor above, which has simple living quarters and a kitchen. The kitchen has no chimney, and the smoke from the wood stove escapes from the windows, leaving behind a thick layer of soot over everything. The top floor is usually a dedicated shrine

room, *choeshum*, which doubles as a guest room.
The airy open attic is used as a drying space or
storage for farm produce. The windows have sliding
wooden shutters. The upper floors are reached by a
steep ladder carved from a tree trunk.

The house opens on to a courtyard, which is used
for daily household activities. The houses of the
wealthy families are larger and elaborately decorated,
with a sizeable enclosed courtyard. Rooms are sparsely
furnished with a few low tables and cupboards. At
night, mattresses are laid on the wooden floor, and
usually the whole family sleeps in the same room.
Pictures of the king and *thangkhas* (scroll paintings)
decorate the walls.

The outer façade
of the house is
whitewashed, and the
timber frames and
windows are painted
black or maroon and
decorated with
colorful traditional
paintings. One
distinct painting is
that of the phallus
(see pages 78-79).
Phallic images adorn
the front walls of
homes, or their
wooden versions
hang from the eaves

to chase away demons, aid fertility, and bring prosperity to the household.

The toilet is separate, built some distance from the main house. In the villages this is usually just a pit in the ground, but Western-style toilets are common in urban houses. Some urban homes now have shower facilities, but bathtubs are rare. Many people still use buckets for everyday washing, as water supplies are erratic; when water is available, containers are filled and stored for future use. In the villages people used to fetch water from springs, often walking miles carrying heavy barrels. Now with the government's effort, almost every village house has access to running water via a tap at the doorstep.

Almost 60 percent of rural areas now have electricity. This has increased the use of electric appliances like electric kettles and rice cookers, although refrigerators and washing machines are hardly used.

Dedicated garbage collection in urban centers means the streets are quite free of litter. However, the excessive chewing of *doma paani* (see page 137) is evident, with smears of lime and unsightly red spit stains everywhere.

FAMILIES—ROLES AND RESPONSIBILITIES

Who the Bhutanese consider "family" depends on the region they come from. Families in western Bhutan tend to be smaller, with strong relationships up to first or second cousins. However, in eastern Bhutan a family can be very extensive, often including cousins as far removed as fifth or sixth.

In Bhutanese families, the roles of parental responsibility are most commonly shared.

Men and women play an equal role in sharing responsibilities for the family. In central Bhutan women are usually the head of the household and decide on the division of labor. There are very few areas where specific work is cut out for each gender. Traditionally, women do most of the everyday household tasks, such as cooking and weaving, while men work out in the fields or perform heavy work, like chopping firewood. But this is not restrictive. Men are equally active in carrying out household duties while women tend to the fields, especially during harvest time, when more hands are in need.

In the urban centers where both husband and wife are employed, the household work is shared. While the wife cooks, the husband will usually take care of the children and their schoolwork. Other chores including laundry, taking children to school, and shopping are shared equally. Most families have a family member such as a grandparent living with them and lending a helping hand. Those who can afford it employ a helper to assist with the duties in the house.

MARRIAGE

Unlike some countries in South Asia, in Bhutan, marriages are not dictated by strict social norms. A wedding can be a completely informal affair or involve an elaborate ceremony. Marriage for love is common, although sometimes a marriage is arranged, with family members or relatives finding someone suitable.

In such cases the potential partners are usually known personally to the family and to each other. However, the couple makes the final decision on the arrangement. It is also common for a couple to move in together and start life as a couple without an official marriage, maybe marrying later.

The wedding is a series of rituals and a ceremony conducted by monks in the monasteries or in the family shrine room in the presence of the family and invited guests. The *tendruel*—solemnizing ceremony—is conducted at an auspicious hour according to astrology. The couple is then presented with a *khadar* (white ceremonial scarf) and gifts, and this is followed by a lavish meal for the gathering. But increasingly people in the towns throw grand, Western-style receptions complete with a wedding cake and a five-course sit-down dinner. In southern Bhutan, marriages are conducted according to Hindu rituals and customs.

Although Bhutan's Marriage Act was passed in 1980, and legal registration of marriage is required by law, it is still not common practice—even less so in the rural areas, where people also tend to marry young (the legal age is eighteen). Most live with their parents even after marriage, and continue to do so with their new family. In rural Bhutan, the husband often moves into his wife's household.

Divorce is on the rise, particularly in urban areas. Adultery and domestic violence are among the major reasons that couples in Bhutan seek to divorce.

NIGHT HUNTING

The term "night hunting" is described as "the traditional Bhutanese custom of courtship" in which a man sneaks into a woman's house and into her bed under the cover of darkness. If the man is found in her bed in the morning, he is accepted formally as her future husband. The woman may have had little or no knowledge of the man's plan to visit her. However, it is entirely up to her to accept or refuse the advances. The refusal would be evident if she alerts the other members of the household, in which case the intruder will be chased out of the house. Opinions about night hunting are completely divided. As practiced commonly in central and eastern Bhutan, many justify it on the grounds that in villages with sparse populations this was a way for young people to find potential partners. Others argue that it is a primitive custom that needs to change with the times. It is also increasingly seen as a means of exploiting vulnerable young girls by men looking for some fun—leading to teenage pregnancies, illegitimate children, and the spread of sexual diseases.

CHILDREN

Children are the center of family life, and the birth of a baby, irrespective of sex, is always a joyous occasion.

When a woman is pregnant, great care is taken to ensure the healthy development of the baby; today, with modern health care, most babies are born in the hospitals. Except for close family members, visitors are discouraged from visiting during the first three days after the birth. On the third day, *lhapsang*—a purification ceremony—is performed by monks in the house, after which the family will receive visitors. In the urban centers, visitors come bearing gifts, such as diapers and children's clothes. In the villages, eggs, meat, and rice are usually brought in as gifts for the mother. A ceremonial scarf, *khadar*, is offered to the baby with a little money to bring good luck.

Directly after giving birth, the mother is encouraged to drink plenty of *changkey* (a porridge-like alcoholic drink) or *ara* (a warm, alcoholic concoction of maize fried in butter and eggs), which is believed to help in the production of breast milk. This beverage is also served to the guests with dried meat and a lot of *eazey* (a salsa-like condiment).

Traditionally, the child is named by a high-ranking monk or the abbot of the local monastery. These days, however, more people take the option of naming their child on their own, or take one given name and combine it with another of their choice. Every child also has a *keytsi*—an individual horoscope—that is drawn up based on the time and date of the birth. The *keytsi* details various rituals to be performed at different stages in the life of the child and also outlines the past and the future of the individual.

Bhutanese children learn to take responsibility from an early age. The older children look after their younger siblings and help them with their schoolwork. Girls assist their mothers with household chores. In the villages, it is common to see children fetching firewood, carrying water, or working in the fields.

EDUCATION

In 1914, forty-six young Bhutanese boys were sent across the border to India to study, and modern education was officially embraced by Bhutan. This was solely the work of Bhutan's first king, Ugyen Wangchuck. The first informal school was established in 1961, and now, more than five decades later, there are 1,926 educational institutions in the country, including monastic schools and adult learning centers.

The system of education in Bhutan is closely related to the Indian system, which was a borrowed system from the British. Both boys and girls are sent to school.

The school-based education comprises eleven years of free basic education. These are divided into seven years of primary education, starting at the age of six, and four years of secondary education, after which students sit the national board exams (Bhutan Certificate for Secondary Education). Those who perform well and score above the percentage set by the education ministry qualify to go on to two more years of preparatory studies before three years of university. Others join the technical training institutes. Some fund their own studies in the few private schools and colleges in the country, or they go abroad, to India or Thailand, for example. But private education is expensive. Parents take out education loans from banks or receive help from family members and relatives, but for a farmer it often means selling land or a prized pair of oxen to fund a child's education.

The academic year begins in mid-February and ends in mid-December, with a month-long summer and winter break, and short breaks between terms. Remote schools in the highlands, where there are long winters, start late and end the academic year earlier than the rest of the country. Books are free, and although most of the schools have boarding facilities, these are limited, so some children in the rural areas still have to walk miles to school every day. English, math, science, history, and geography are taught in schools in both English and Dzongkha. Currently 98 percent of children attend primary school, indicating that Bhutan is close to achieving the goal of universal primary education.

Urban centers like Thimphu and Paro have seen major growth in primary education. There are now many private kindergartens and elite primary schools. There are numerous scholarship programs for higher studies provided by the government for bright students. Many are sent to study engineering, medicine, and law to neighboring countries on full scholarship. Adult learning centers provide basic education to those keen to learn to read and write.

EMPLOYMENT

Besides agriculture, which engages 57 percent of the population, the government is the largest employer in Bhutan. To become a civil servant is no small feat. The respect and prestige that come with the position also appeal to the majority. This also plays on to the concept of *tha-damtsi*, where being in the government service is equated to being in the direct service of the *Tsa-Wa-Sum*—"king, country, and people."

Civil servants are, no doubt, powerful and play an important role in the development of the country. Young graduates enter a series of competitive entrance exams, and the successful candidates are enrolled in a rigorous training program with further opportunities to move into different ministries and departments. Those graduates who succeed in the examinations are seen as the smartest and brightest of all, and many young people study with the sole aim of getting through them.

At non-graduate levels, young people compete through open competition for posts in the government. However, of late the government bureaucracy has become huge, and its intake relative to the number of graduates has been decreasing, with many having to look at the private sector, which is still in its infancy and not the first choice of employment.

Working for a corporation or a big company is the second choice, and salaries are comparatively higher than in the civil service. With the government privatizing a number of sectors in recent years, it is likely that people will start to look more favorably at the private sector. In addition, there are many small entrepreneurs and programs run by the government and NGOs that have immensely helped to change perceptions in recent years.

The cost of living is high, especially in the urban areas, and many middle-class families struggle to make ends meet. People often have two jobs or find ways to bring in extra money. A civil servant might drive a taxi on weekends and after office hours. Housewives boost the family income by weaving at home or running a grocery shop.

Unemployment is a rising issue in the urban areas. The National Statistics Bureau places Bhutan's youth unemployment rate at around 10 percent— one of the highest in the region. A major contribution is rural–urban migration. Young people leave their villages and flock to the towns in search of work and a better life. There are reports of entire villages being abandoned or left only to the old and the vulnerable. There is even a term, *goongtong* (empty houses), to describe the phenomenon.

HEALTH CARE

As with education, Bhutan provides free health care services to its citizens. Modern health care was established in the early 1960s, and since then Bhutan has made remarkable progress, with primary health care covering more than 90 per cent of the population. There are three well-equipped referral hospitals in Thimphu, Gelephu, and Mongar, and one hospital in each of the twenty districts except Gasa. Basic health units (BHU) and outreach clinics bring health to remote areas. Patients in need of sophisticated and expensive treatments are referred abroad at government expense.

Bhutan's life expectancy is sixty-eight years: a great advance from thirty-seven years in 1960. Major progress has been made in lowering the infant mortality rate, which was at an alarming level of 103 per 1,000 live births in 1984. In 2018 the rate was 24.8 per 1,000 live births. Child immunization is above 90 percent, and access to potable water and public sanitation has improved over the years. A big chunk of government expenditure (7–11 percent of the total expenditure) has been on health. Bhutan is one of the few countries that are well on their way to achieving the UN Millennium Development Goals (MDGs).

But challenges remain: rising health care expenditure, a perennial shortage of doctors and other medical staff, and the changing needs of the population. One particular challenge to public health has been the increase in lifestyle diseases such as type 2 diabetes, heart disease, stroke, and hypertension.

With increasing pressure on the free system, the government has encouraged the growth of private health consultancies and clinics in recent years for those willing to pay for their services.

TRADITIONAL MEDICINE

Traditional Bhutanese medicine, or *Sowa Rigpa*, is an important part of health care in Bhutan. A renowned Tibetan physician, Tenzin Drukey, is credited with having brought *Sowa Rigpa* to Bhutan in the early seventeenth century when he arrived with the Zhabdrung. Tibetans referred to Bhutan as *Lhomen Jong*—the "Land of Medicinal Herbs." In the following centuries, many Bhutanese travelled to Tibet to train and study from their Tibetan counterparts, and in exchange they took with them various medicinal plants found in the high mountains of Bhutan. Upon return, the qualified *drungtshos* (traditional healers) set up practices in monasteries and *dzongs* across the country. Traditional medicine soon rose in prominence

DAILY LIFE AND ROUTINE

The Bhutanese are early risers. In the villages, the household chores are done and breakfast is eaten by the time the sun is up. In the urban centers, the working day starts early, beginning with prayers and offering of *yoenchap* (clean water in bowls, a butter lamp, and burning of incense sticks) at the family altar. Breakfast is a simple meal of rice, *eazey*—a mixture of chopped green/dried chili, onion, tomato, coriander with the support of the royal family, and in 1968 the first dispensary was opened in Thimphu. A decade later the institute was established in what is now called the Faculty of Traditional Medicine.

Traditional medicine is a holistic and inclusive combination of art, science, and philosophy. The condition is diagnosed with reading of the pulses and examining the color of the eyes, tongue, urine, and face. Daily diet and lifestyle are taken into account. Treatment procedures include golden needle therapy (acupuncture), extraction of diseased blood (cupping/moxibustion), hot oil compression, herbal steaming, and bathing. There is also medication in powder or syrup form made from fine combinations of thousands of medicinal plants, minerals, and some animal parts.

and *datsi* (local cheese)—and butter tea. Toast, eggs, and cereals are popular among younger people.

Parents drop their children at school at 8:00 a.m. and go to work. Office hours are from 9:00 a.m. to 5:00 p.m., or 4:00 p.m. in winter for government offices. General stores (or grocery shops, as they are called) open early, but regular shops follow the office times. Most people drive to work, and many walk. In Thimphu the city buses provide a good service for those living in the suburbs.

The lunch hour is from 1:00 p.m. to 2:00 p.m. Most office workers bring food with them and eat together with their colleagues; there may also be an office cafeteria. Some people go home for lunch, and young breastfeeding mothers will return home at this time to feed their babies. Children take packed lunches to school.

School finishes at 3:30 p.m., and most children walk home, ambling along with large groups of friends. Once home, they usually sit down and do their homework. and then watch TV. People with families usually go home after work, but young adults go out with friends or play sports.

Supper is the main meal of the day, and meal times are considered important for getting together. Most families eat together, sitting cross-legged on the floor in a circle, with the food placed in the middle. Western-style dining tables are common in urban households. It is usually the women who serve the food—in most cases the mother of the family. A typical meal will include a mountain of rice with one or two stews (meat or vegetable, or both), with *eazey* as a common accompaniment. Traditionally, rice is eaten with the right hand, pressed into small balls and dipped in the bowl of stew. Spoons are widely used now. The rice and the stew are not mixed together, as one sees in India or Nepal, where the curry is mixed well with rice. The variety of dishes served at meals is different in different households, depending on status. The traditional bamboo-woven and wooden bowls have fast disappeared, replaced by cheap and convenient melamine products imported from Bangladesh.

After clearing up, the family usually sits down to watch TV. All activities cease by 9:00 p.m. Shops close, and streets are deserted as everyone winds down for the day.

SHOPPING

Shopping in Bhutan is an entirely different experience from shopping in the West. There are no giant supermarket chains or department stores where one

Thimphu central market.

can find everything under one roof. It is only in Thimphu that you will find some Western-style shopping centers (hardly malls by any standard) with a few choices of goods available. There are a few mini marts that provide imported packaged and canned foods, such as pasta, biscuits, chocolates, dried fruits, and sauces, which are mostly from India and Thailand. These are, however, expensive beyond the reach of most Bhutanese.

In most towns, weekly vegetable shopping is done at local farmers' markets, which are set up for the weekends. They sell everything from locally produced vegetables, fruit, and meat to local cheese and butter, eggs, dried vegetables, and dried fish. Imported vegetables from India are also sold, which are cheaper in comparison. However, the importation of some Indian vegetables, on which a high presence of pesticides was found, has been banned in recent years, resulting in vegetable shortages and price hikes. Some Bhutanese now use online apps and services for deliveries of their shopping. These apps are yet to become an everyday feature of Bhutanese shopping habits, however.

In smaller towns, villagers come once a week to sell their fresh produce. The market is set up at dawn, and if you don't hurry you'll return empty-handed. People stock up on supplies for the week, and for other food items they buy from general stores. You will see goods still on sale past their sell-by date, especially in smaller towns and village shops.

Most general stores sell just about everything—from clothes, shoes, bags, and beauty products to children's toys—and it's difficult to move around without bumping into piles of things or knocking them over. If you don't see what you want, ask—if you can pry the salesperson away from the small TV in the corner. Customer service can leave much to be desired.

Online shopping has made inroads in Bhutan in recent years and many now use online ecommerce platforms that are based in India, such as Amazon India, Flipkart, Myntra, and Snapdeal, as well as those in China, such as AliExpress. These companies will deliver the products to the nearest border town and either the customer will collect the item directly, or they will arrange for a local Bhutanese company to deliver it to them. In addition, Facebook Marketplace has also become quite popular for the buying and selling of used items.

CHAPTER SIX

TIME OUT

Unlike the situation in the West, where people look forward to an exciting or relaxing weekend after a week of hard work, the Bhutanese generally do not make many plans for their leisure time. While government offices are closed on weekends, schools and private offices have half days on Saturdays. Most families spend their Saturdays shopping for fresh vegetables and other food items at the weekend markets, dealing with their laundry, and cleaning the house. Friends and relatives may drop by unannounced for an impromptu get-together during weekends or even on weekdays. In the urban areas, young people gather in the local cafés or snooker rooms to chat and play games, or meet up in the shopping malls in the bigger towns such as Thimphu and Phuentsholing.

EATING OUT

The Bhutanese have never been big on eating out, which was strictly reserved for celebrating special occasions, and restaurants catered mainly to tourists. This is changing in urban centers with the improved standard of living and a growing number of young professionals adopting a Western lifestyle. A number of restaurants now also deliver food.

Bhutanese cuisine is interesting but limited. Beside the rice, stews, and meat and vegetable curries, there is not a great deal of variety, unlike Indian and Chinese cuisines with their vast choices. However, with modernization and a thriving tourism industry much has changed over the years. The hotels have worked with international tourism professionals to train their chefs and kitchen staff to improve the variety and standard of food served.

As a result of these efforts and the growing number of imports from India and other neighboring countries, people living in the urban areas now have access to different cuisines—largely categorized as Indian, Chinese, and Western Continental, and heavily influenced by one another. One may come across Chinese dishes such as a Chicken Chili or a Chicken Manchurian, both Indo-Chinese dishes that are popular in South Asia. Among the specialties, Tibetan *momos*—steamed or fried dumplings, stuffed with meat or vegetables, and *thukpa* or *bathup* (noodle soup)—are popular, with every restaurant in town serving them with a hot chili sauce. They are usually eaten as a quick snack or as a meal in itself.

Tibetan-styled momo dumplings, a local favorite.

One can enjoy a variety of dishes, often fused with Bhutanese elements. *Kewa-datsi* (potato and cheese) and *shamu-datsi* (mushroom and cheese) are popular milder versions of the all-chili dish (see below), which are often better suited to a foreigner's palate. It may come as a surprise to a Westerner to be served rice with potato stew, a favorite of the locals ("carbs on carbs," as an amused British tourist remarked).

Most imported foods are from India and Thailand, the latter being the preferred choice of most Bhutanese for their quality and variety. However, the product labels are in Thai and not easily readable by the Bhutanese. Locally manufactured "Western" food, such as "Swiss cheese" (which tastes like English cheddar or Dutch gouda), honey, and jam are available in stores.

All meals for tourists are usually prearranged in restaurants that have high standards and overall good hygiene and have been approved by the Tourism

Council. Packed lunches are prepared for day hikes or long drives, especially when you travel farther east, where chances of finding good restaurants along the way are few and far between.

TIPPING

Tipping is purely a personal matter. There is no tradition of giving tips as part of a commercial transaction, such as in a restaurant or after a taxi ride. However, giving *soelra* may be a Bhutanese practice closest to tipping. *Soelra* directly translates as a reward given by an elder or your boss as an appreciation for hard work and dedication. If you would like to show your appreciation and tip your tour guide and driver, they will appreciate it. Some restaurants now include a service charge on the bill, which is generally between 10 and 15 percent, and some hotels have a box for tips at the front desk.

BHUTANESE FOOD

A common thread that runs through all of Bhutan is the use of chili peppers—an important food ingredient for all Bhutanese. The jalapeno pepper variety is the one generally used. The national dish of Bhutan, *ema-datsi*, is made entirely of chilies. Chilies, fresh or dried, are simply split lengthwise and boiled in little water with a tablespoon or two of butter, salt, and scallions, and mixed with the local cheese called *datsi* (similar to feta cheese but without the salt). Fermented beans and strong-smelling moldy cheese (called *zoedey* or *yeotpa*) are delicacies in some regions of western and eastern Bhutan.

Air-dried meat is a specialty among the Drukpas. It is common to see strips of meat hung from windows or placed on the rooftops to air or sun-dry, along with ripe chili peppers. Thinly sliced dried belly pork, *phaksha pa*, is a special dish served during feasts. Yak meat is a staple diet for the highlanders, and chicken and mutton are commonly eaten in the south. Fresh fish is occasionally available from the local rivers, although there are strict regulations around fishing. Most of the fish served has been imported from the neighboring Indian state of West Bengal. Dried fish, cooked with dried red chilies and potatoes, is a delicacy. Eggs are also an integral part of the diet, usually hardboiled or scrambled.

The Bhutanese are good at foraging. Wild mushrooms, tender bamboo shoots, fiddlehead ferns (young, furled fern fronds), nettle flowers, orchid flower buds, and other edible plants are enjoyed by the locals. *Doma paani*—areca nut and betel leaves with a dash of slaked lime—is offered at the end of a meal, mostly to aid digestion. To offer *doma paani* to friends or even strangers is to express friendship, or is a polite social gesture.

DRINKS

The local *ara,* made from maize with a 20 percent alcohol content, is a popular drink—even more so in eastern Bhutan, where the day begins with a nice dose of it with breakfast before tending the fields. *Suja* and *nga ja*—Tibetan-style salt butter tea, and Indian-style tea with milk and sugar, respectively— are popular hot drinks. A few cafés in Thimphu and Paro now serve decent filter coffee, a long step from the days of "instant coffee only."

Various brands of alcoholic drinks from India and Thailand are popular, as well as locally produced Red Panda beer, Special Courier, and Black Mountain whiskeys. The larger shops may sell, expensively, a few varieties of imported wines similar to those found cheaply in supermarket aisles in the West. More choices are available in the only duty-free shop in Thimphu, but these are out of reach for most locals. Drinks are always accompanied with spicy snacks and local *eazey*—the salsa-like condiment of chopped chilies, tomatoes, onions, coriander, and fresh cottage cheese.

PICNICS

The Bhutanese spend much of their leisure time at home with their family. However, once in a while they like to go out for a picnic with family, friends, or colleagues. During bank holidays, especially on an auspicious day, most families go on an excursion to visit a remote monastery and take along a picnic lunch to enjoy in the woods. The picnic lunch is a lavish affair with rice and a variety of meat and vegetable curries packed in large hot cases, and tall flasks of hot drinks and bottles of local wine and other drinks, all carefully packed and carried in rucksacks. The more adventurous go on a "wild picnic," carrying cooking utensils so they can cook food from scratch in the open air.

Picnic outings are usually accompanied by loudspeakers blaring the latest local and Bollywood music. Traditional games of archery and darts (*khuru;* see page 142) usually end the day.

WHAT TO WEAR

The national dresses—*gho* and *kira*—are worn to offices, business meetings, and to schools by all Bhutanese. It is also mandatory that everyone wears the ceremonial scarves while entering government buildings with the national flag. Foreigners and tourists need not comply with the strict dress codes while visiting the *dzongs* and monasteries, but they are required to dress decently—no Bermuda shorts or sleeveless shirts, and no short skirts for women. You will need to remove shoes and hats while visiting monasteries and temples.

VACATIONS AND PUBLIC HOLIDAYS

It may come as a surprise to foreigners that traditionally there is no concept of "going on vacation" in Bhutan. The notion of breaking free from the daily routine and setting aside time to spend large amounts of money on relaxing and traveling for pleasure is completely alien to older Bhutanese. The closest parallel to a vacation is when office employees take a week off to travel to their home in the village for the annual religious ceremonies called. Also, every winter, families will make pilgrimages to Buddhist sites in India and Nepal. The vacation concept is, however, picking up among the younger generation. Families who can afford it take family vacations to neighboring countries like Nepal, India, and Thailand.

However, Bhutan enjoys a fair amount of public holidays each year—an average of twenty-one days annually, celebrating the birth anniversaries of the kings, Buddhist religious days, and various festivals, as described in Chapter 3.

SPORTS AND EXERCISE

Bhutan's national sport is archery, which is much loved and popular with all age groups. Competitive tournaments are held year-round, throughout the country. In Thimphu different government offices form teams, and compete for the coveted

championship cup and prizes. Archery is the only sport in which Bhutan has consistently participated at the Olympics since 1984. The traditional bow and arrows, while still in use in the rural areas, have given way to the more sophisticated modern imported compound bows. Each team player aims to hit two targets placed 476 feet (145 m) apart.

An archery tournament is a social event. It begins with a ceremony, and food and drinks are served throughout. When a player scores a *karey* (hits the target) his team members celebrate with a coordinated dance and song in praise of his skill. Women participate as cheerleaders, singing and taunting an opponent archer to distract him from his aim.

Khuru (a darts game) is another traditional sport, played wherever there is an open space. The darts are homemade—usually a nail hammered into a little

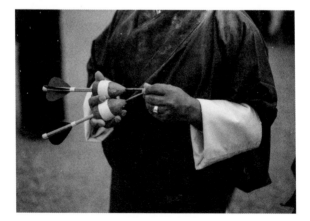

block of wood, with feathers attached—and aimed at a small target, typically a rectangular piece of wood placed on the ground some sixty feet (about 18 m) away.

Other sports, such as football, basketball, cricket, and tennis, are also played. Football and basketball are the favorites, with many clubs and teams emerging in the urban areas. International football events like the World Cup and English Premier League are closely followed on TV. Golf is played among the elite and the upper middle class. There is only one public golf course in the country, located in Thimphu.

Exercising for health is an emerging cultural trend. With lifestyle diseases like diabetes on the rise, more and more Bhutanese consider it essential to keep fit. A number of health clubs are now operating in Thimphu. You will see people walking, jogging, and cycling along the road and in parks in the morning, and there are open-air gyms at various locations around the city to encourage people to exercise and get moving. Also, Bhutan's pristine environment, lush green forests, gushing rivers, and rolling mountains are an ideal setting for adrenalin-pumping outdoor adventures such as trekking, mountain biking, river rafting, and kayaking.

Trekking

Trekking in Bhutan is different from elsewhere in the Himalayas. Step off the beaten path, and you are in a world that seems untouched and unseen. Peace and solitude reign. There are no hotels or lodges; instead, you camp at designated camping sites with yaks and yak herders for company. A team—guide, cook, and assistant cook—accompanies you on the trek, cooking you fresh meals and helping to set up the tents. Your tour company provides all the trekking equipment, such as foam mattresses, eating utensils, and dining and toilet tents. Horses or yaks in the higher regions do the carrying.

The trails wind across rugged mountains, with steep climbs and sudden descents, and pass through various zones of vegetation, from broadleaf forests to alpine meadows. There are views of breathtaking landscapes, and most of the trails are in protected parks, so you may chance upon wild animals in their natural habitats. The most popular trekking routes are the paths of varying lengths to the base of Mount Jomolhari, passing through the highland communities of Laya and Lingzhi, and those in the lush valleys of Bumthang, in central Bhutan. The world's arguably most treacherous trek, aptly named the "Snowman's Trek," leads across the remote Lunana region, and on this trek you camp in the snow at heights of nearly 16,500 feet (approx. 5,000 m).

Mountain Biking

The tourism industry recognized mountain biking as a viable attraction a few years ago, and since then it has gained considerable popularity with both locals and visitors. A number of dedicated trails are located in Phobjikha and Punakha, and similar cycling excursions are possible in Paro, Thimphu, and Bumthang, with its beautiful wide valleys. For those wanting to experience more, a cross-country biking tour takes you along a winding highway, which involves a lot of uphill pedaling and negotiation of sharp bends and corners. The Tour of the Dragon Bicycle Race, held every year in early September, covers 167 miles (268 km), with contestants pedaling along the highway over four high mountain passes between Bumthang and Thimphu.

Whitewater Rafting

Although most of Bhutan's fast-running rivers and deep gorges are unsuitable for whitewater rafting, some are being considered as potential sites for some of the best river rafting in the world. The easy, gentle float on the Mo Chhu River in Punakha stretches to around six miles (approx. 10 km), starting at the Khamsum Yuelley Namgyal Chorten point and ending past the Punakha Dzong; it has few rapids, and is popular with locals and visitors alike. The Pho Chhu River provides a similar-length course comprising ten rapids and amazing scenery as you float along.

CULTURAL AND SOCIAL LIFE

Nightlife

There is generally little to do after dark in Bhutan. People go home early, and by 9:00 p.m. everything has closed down and the streets are deserted. In Thimphu, however, bars and nightclubs remain open late on weekends, and on Friday night young locals gather to dance and party, with DJs playing a fusion of the latest dance music that is popular around the world. These clubs are quite small, with modest dance floors, and are rarely crowded.

Dance and Music

Traditional dance and music are an integral part of Bhutanese culture. Buddhist mask dances (*cham*) performed to chants and rhythmic music depict Buddhist teachings and fables at various religious festivals (*tshechus*). A long horn (*dungchen*), an oboe (*gyaling*), a bell (*drilbu*), and a double-sided drum (*nga*) beaten with a curved stick are some of the instruments that form the core orchestra for religious music.

Secular music and folksongs are greatly influenced by the Buddhist tradition and the classical Tibetan style of music called *boedra*. Another popular style of singing is *zhungdra*. Traditional musical instruments such as the Bhutanese lute (*dranyen*), the bamboo flute (*lym*), and the two-stringed violin played with a single bowstring (*chiwang*) create melodious tunes. In the south, traditional Nepali instruments such as the *madal*, a two-headed hand drum, are popular.

In the last two decades, the modern, Western-inspired Bhutanese songs called *rigsar* have gained tremendous popularity among the locals. These are accompanied by instruments such as guitar, drums, and electric synthesizer. They are heavily influenced by Western pop culture and Indian Bollywood music. Many singers and bands are releasing albums that are well received by the public.

Cinema

Bhutan's small film industry is fairly new, but it is thriving. Movies are made in the native Dzongkha language; the plots are largely based on folklore, legends, and history, with song and dance sequences, like old Hollywood musicals and the more modern Bollywood movies. The first Dzongkha movie ever made was the 1989 *Gasa Lamai Singye*, and since then more than a hundred movies have been produced and screened in the country.

The few cinemas in Bhutan are only allowed to screen local films. For a long time, the only cinema in Thimphu was the now renovated Lugar Theater. In the last few years, a number of new cinemas have opened in the capital with better seats and sound systems. The Trowa Theater, Ninda Bescope, City Cinema, and the new Luger Theater run full houses with local movies.

Young, independent filmmakers now take their works to international festivals and have won accolades. The most popular Bhutanese maker is Kyentse Norbu, who is also a revered incarnate lama. His first movie, *Phorba* (*The Cup*, 1999), was popular in the festival circle, and his second, *Travellers and Magicians* (2005, in Dzongkha with English subtitles), won awards at various international festivals.

The industry has its own awards—the National Film Awards—that honor the best movies and performances of the year.

Museums and Galleries

Bhutan does not have the long-established museum and gallery culture of Europe, but there are a few museums and privately run galleries in Thimphu and Paro. Ta Dzong, the National Museum of Bhutan in Paro, houses a collection of rare and important artifacts, such as the large "horse egg." Another popular museum in Thimpu is the National Textile Museum. The museum explores Bhutan's rich and long-standing traditions of *thagzo* (weaving) and *tshemzo* (embroidery), and showcases both ancient and modern pieces.

Bhutanese art is heavily influenced by Buddhism. Elaborate and exquisite paintings depicting Buddhist teachings and fables adorn the walls of monasteries.

The Voluntary Artists' Studio (VAST) is popular, and promotes contemporary art and talented artists among the youth of the country. It was founded in 1998 by the veteran artist Kama Wangdi, fondly called Asha (maternal uncle) Kama by his students. The GoldOm Creatives gallery in Changangkha is also worth visiting.

CHANGING MONEY

Bhutan's currency is the ngultrum (Nu.). This is pegged to and at par with the Indian rupee, which is legal tender.

Travelers' checks in US dollars are still in use, but it's best to carry cash—preferably US dollars—and easiest to change it to the local currency in Thimphu, as facilities are almost nonexistent in the interior. You can change money at Paro airport on arrival, at banks in the major towns, and at a couple of authorized outlets in Thimphu. You can also withdraw cash from ATMs using Visa or MasterCard, but charges are high.

Other currencies acceptable for exchange are the pound sterling, euro, Japanese yen, Swiss franc, Canadian dollar, Hong Kong dollar, Danish, Swedish, and Norwegian kroners, and Australian and Singapore dollars. Visa, MasterCard, and American Express credit cards are accepted in the larger handicraft shops and many hotels.

HANDICRAFTS

Many of Bhutan's traditional arts and crafts (*zorig chusum*) continue today, in the production of everyday objects for use by the locals. They include painting,

sculpture, cast metalwork, woodwork, weaving, and papermaking. There are handicraft shops in all major towns, and the handicraft market lane in Thimphu sells products from all over the country. Note that bargaining is not customary and is best not attempted.

Fine textiles and local handicrafts are the best buys when it comes to shopping for souvenirs and gifts. Handwoven fabrics such as sheep's and yak's wool (*yathra*) from Bumthang, raw silk (*bura*) from Trashigang, and the intricately designed *kusuthara* from Lhuentse are a hit with the visitors. Used mainly for clothing locally, these rich textiles are now also made into handbags, men's ties, and jackets, which sell well. *Thangkhas* (scroll paintings) depicting Buddhist themes and scenes from folklore, and especially of the *Thuenpa Puenzhi* ("Four Harmonious Friends"), can be expensive, but depend on the quality and experience of the painter.

Bhutanese jewelry is chunky and striking. Coral and turquoise are used abundantly, in gold and silver settings. Wooden bowls (*dapa*) and cane and bamboo containers (*bangchung*) are popular too, along with many small ornamental items.

There are gilt brass and copper statues, mostly of Buddhist deities and ritual objects; but most of these are modern imports from Nepal. The export of genuine antique statues and artifacts is strictly prohibited unless clearance is given by the Cultural Department, and this can be difficult to obtain.

Some of Bhutan's national stamps are highly prized by collectors. You can buy these in sets at the main post office in Thimphu and Phuentsholing.

CHAPTER SEVEN

TRAVEL, HEALTH, & SAFETY

VISAS

All foreigners (except visitors from Bangladesh, India, and the Maldives) will need a visa before their arrival. There are no facilities to obtain visas from any of Bhutan's missions abroad. Independent travelers are not allowed at present. All tourists must arrange their visits either through a local Bhutanese tour operator or through one of their international partner agencies. Tours are all operated on a pre-paid basis, and visas are arranged by the tour operator. A copy of the visa clearance number with the approved itinerary is issued to your tour operator who will, in turn, send it to you. You will have to produce a printout of the visa copy at the point of entry (airports and border towns if traveling by road), along with your plane tickets and a passport with a validity of more than six months. Official guests have their arrangements made on their behalf by their host ministry, department, or organization before their arrival. The visa is issued within two working days.

Visa extension of a maximum of six months can be applied in Thimphu, but this service is available only to long-term expatriates or those in residence. For tourists, if unavoidable circumstances such as bad weather or roadblocks warrant a stay longer than the permitted duration, no visa extension is required.

There is a small community of expatriates in Bhutan, consisting mainly of people working for the different UN organizations, the bilateral and multilateral development partner countries, and some volunteers and experts working for various government and non-profit organizations. If any government or private organizations wish to employ a foreigner, approval must be sought from the Department of Labour for a valid work permit. Very few foreign individuals who have contributed significantly to Bhutan and have made Bhutan their home have been granted residential visas.

HIGH-VALUE, LOW-IMPACT TOURISM

Tourism in Bhutan is governed by a policy of "high value, low impact," which means that tourism must be "environmentally and ecologically friendly, socially and culturally acceptable, and economically viable." Tour operators must abide by strict regulations set by the tourism board. A minimum daily tariff of US $250 per person is applicable for those traveling during the peak seasons of spring and autumn; for the off-peak months of January, February, June to August, and December, the daily tariff is US $200. The tariff covers basic accommodation, meals, guide, sightseeing, and transport. For a group of fewer than three persons there is an additional daily surcharge. US $65 is deducted from the daily tariff as a "sustainable development fee," which is used by the government toward free education, free health care, and building infrastructure. There are discounts for stays of a longer duration.

However, with this policy there is a common misunderstanding that Bhutan is an expensive destination and restricts the number of people coming into the country.

TRAVELING TO BHUTAN

Traveling to Bhutan is not easy, and the best way is to fly. The only international airport in Bhutan is in Paro. Flights are with the national airline, Druk Air, and the privately owned Bhutan Airlines. Druk Air flies to and from Bangkok (Thailand), Kathmandu (Nepal), Singapore, Dhaka (Bangladesh), and the Indian cities of New Delhi, Kolkata, Gaya, Bagdogra, and Guwahati. Bhutan Airlines currently flies to and from Bangkok, Kathmandu, and Delhi. There are limited flights, which operate only during the day, and the schedule changes every season. Early bookings are recommended during the peak months of spring

A Royal Bhutan Airlines (Druk Air) flight disembarks at Paro Airport.

(mid-February to early May) and autumn (mid-September to mid-November). It is advisable to book tours at least four to six months in advance. Avoid arranging tight connections, and note that it is best to stay overnight at the gateway city before catching your onward flight to Paro.

Flying into Paro is not for the fainthearted. Descents are sudden and awkward as the plane negotiates its way through the high mountains and over the rooftops before landing, but the fresh air and serene surroundings are welcome after the chaotic din of the cities. Guides will receive guests at the airport, most

often with the traditional welcoming offer of a *khadar*—the white scarf.

You can also travel over land from India through one of the border towns of Phuentsholing or Samdrupjongkhar in southern Bhutan. The nearest airport to Phuentsholing is a four-hour drive away in Bagdogra, West Bengal, while Guwahati airport in Assam is a three-hour drive away from Samdrupjongkhar. Both of these Indian airports have daily flights from New Delhi and other Indian cities. Your tour operator can arrange your transport from these airports.

URBAN TRANSPORTATION

Public transportation in the urban centers is almost nonexistent, except for city buses in a few of the bigger towns, such as Thimphu, Paro, and Phuentsholing. The smaller towns have no public transportation facilities. The majority of the people drive around in their own vehicles, or on scooters or motorbikes, and many just walk. Driving is on the left side of the road, and traffic rules are strictly followed, with regular checks for up-to-date papers conducted by the traffic police. For tourists, all transportation is provided as part of the tour package. If you bring your own vehicle through the border you will need a special permit, and your tour operator can process this for you. Indian nationals can drive around in their own vehicles as long as all necessary papers are in place and endorsed by the road safety and transport authority (RSTA).

Except for buses in bigger towns such as Paro (pictured), public transportation in Bhutan is scarce.

CITY BUSES

Thimphu city, spread across ten square miles
(26 sq. km), is well covered by buses, and most
operate until 10:00 p.m. E-tickets can be bought
from designated outlets. Some buses accept fares
paid to the conductor before the journey. It is a
cheap mode of transport for many, and is used
mainly by locals, office workers, and school students.
During peak hours buses are crowded and the
timetable is unreliable, which can leave commuters
waiting for hours with no sign of a bus.

PRIVATE VEHICLES

Bhutan imports all its vehicles. Japanese, Korean,
and Indian cars are popular choices. Earlier, most
of these were old cars, but now all kinds of new and
expensive cars are imported. Although traffic jams
like those found in the big cities of neighboring
countries are unheard of, the increasing number of
vehicles, especially in Thimphu (the city alone has
over 52,000 vehicles, almost half of the total
registered in the country), has led to the creation of
one-way streets and roadside parking charged on an
hourly basis in the city center. During the morning
and evening rush hours the traffic is slow, and it is
nearly impossible to find a convenient parking spot.
   Measures taken by the government to limit the
increase of vehicles, such as heavy import duties and

the introduction of fuel taxes, have only been partially successful. Electric cars are encouraged as an alternative but, aside from a few electric taxis, these have yet to catch on.

TAXIS

Taxis have a distinctive yellow band across the top of the vehicle and can be easily hailed in the streets or at designated spots. Those with green driving plates are fully electric. Fares are fixed according to the destination, are not negotiable, and are quite

expensive by local standards. Taxis also operate long-distance between towns on a shared ride. You can hire a taxi on your own or with others to share the cost. New ride-hailing apps such as DrukRide and Oie Drive have recently begun operating in and around Thimphu.

GETTING AROUND THE COUNTRY

Only recently Druk Air started twice-weekly flights from Paro to Jakar in central Bhutan and to Gelephu in the south. These are used mostly by tourists looking to cut down on the road travel time. Only a few Bhutanese can afford air travel, and the rest generally drive themselves or take buses.

Traveling by road is the primary way to make any journey in Bhutan. The first motorable road, the Phuentsholing–Thimphu Highway, was completed in 1961. Since then, a good network of roads connects most of the regions and towns; remote villages are accessible by farm roads. The East–West, or Lateral, Highway traverses the country from Thimphu in the west to Trashigang in the east, passing through and connecting the four districts of Wangduephodrang, Trongsa, Bumthang, and Mongar. The rest of the national highways branch out from these regions. Another easy travel option to the east is through India in the south. Road improvement is a priority for the government. The Thimphu–Phuentsholing Highway has a double lane

The breathtaking scenery of the lower Himalayas.

now, and the Lateral Highway is undergoing
expansion.

Road travel in Bhutan is a long, slow, and tiring
experience, with the narrow, single lanes, numerous
sharp bends, and seemingly endless steep ascents and
descents. You have to wait patiently behind heavily
laden trucks trundling along the narrow stretches until
they can let you pass. The average speed for road travel
rarely exceeds 25 miles per hour (40 kmph)—less if

conditions are bad. The arduous ride is, however,
generously rewarded by spectacular scenery of
green valleys and farmhouses scattered across the
mountainside.

Except for some of the highways in western Bhutan,
traffic on the highway is almost negligible. It may
be a while before you see another car on the road.
Mountain roads are always unpredictable, and it is
important to allow plenty of time for your journey.

There are frequent roadblocks, caused by landslides
in the monsoon season and by winter snow (in the
higher altitudes). The delays can sometimes be
severe, leading up to days without access.

Buses

Long-distance buses are a lifeline for the majority of
Bhutanese. There are regular buses from Thimphu to
the other towns of Paro, Punakha, Wangduephodrang,
and Phuentsholing, and fewer to other parts of the
country, such as Bumthang and Samtse in the south.
There is also a direct bus twice a week from Thimphu
to Trashigang in the east, which is a two-day journey
with a night halt in Bumthang, covering roughly
350 miles (562 km).

The big, rattly, Indian-made buses have all been
replaced by more comfortable Toyota Coaster buses
and minibuses. The buses are cheap, but with the
huge demand it is important to book tickets in
advance. Strict road regulations mean the buses are
not overcrowded. It can, however, get a bit messy,
as many passengers suffer motion sickness. There
have been stories of people throwing up all over the
floor or, worse, on to the hapless passenger in front
of them.

Even so, a long road journey can be interesting.
The latest Bhutanese and Bollywood songs blaring
from the speakers above will keep you entertained.
It is easy to strike up a conversation with your fellow
passengers, and it is always polite to offer or share
snacks or food.

Hitchhiking

Another popular mode of travel is hitchhiking, especially in central and eastern Bhutan. It is common for people to flag down cars for a ride, and it is equally common for a Bhutanese to give a lift to someone in need. These are generally free rides, but trucks plying the road often charge people. In the remote parts of the country, tractors and other farm vehicles come in handy for hitching.

Tourist Vehicles

Tourist transportation is included in the pre-booked package—usually medium-sized or minibuses, such as Toyota Coaster and Hiace buses, or four-wheel-drive vehicles for smaller groups. Travel in Bhutan involves a lot of time spent on the road, so a comfortable vehicle is often a necessity more than a luxury. Most of these vehicles are well stocked with cushions and blankets to make your travel as comfortable as the winding, bumpy roads allow.

WHERE TO STAY

Tourism regulations require that all tourists be accommodated in a hotel with a minimum of three stars that is registered and recognized by the tourism board. This ensures a good standard of service and that tour companies do not compromise on quality. Hostels for tourists are nonexistent. There are a couple of youth hostels in Thimphu, which are used

Accomodation at the Six Senses Lodge in Thimphu.

by local students and young people only.

In major tourist regions and towns like Thimphu, Paro, Punakha, and Bumthang, there is a good choice of hotels, ranging from high-end luxury to basic three-star hotels. However, during the peak festival seasons of spring and fall, hotels get booked up very fast, and it becomes extremely difficult to find rooms. Reputable hotels with good services are booked well in advance—sometimes a year ahead. It is always a challenge for tour companies to find hotels of choice for late bookings. Indian nationals traveling on their own can make bookings directly with the hotels. Many hotels take credit-card payments, although most operate on cash payments only.

As you travel further east, accommodation becomes more basic and limited. There are small hotels, often family run, with a few basic rooms and shared bathrooms. Homestays and farmhouse stays with local families are encouraged to give extra income to the farmers and also provide you with an authentic, up-close experience of Bhutanese rural life. When making your travel bookings, you can specify your interest to stay in a farmhouse, and your tour company will make the arrangement.

Trekking in Bhutan is completely in the wilderness. Unlike Nepal, Bhutan has no mountain lodges where you can spend the night after a day's walk; instead, you camp out, often alongside yak herders and their yaks. Camping spots are marked along the major trekking routes. Your team's cook and assistants walk on ahead to set up the tents and prepare everything for the night. Delicious hot meals are served, and hot shower facilities are also provided.

HEALTH AND SAFETY

Visit your doctor or a travel clinic at least eight weeks before departure for general advice on travel risks in the region, and ensure all your basic vaccinations and boosters are up to date. Also, check current requirements with your travel company. It is necessary to vaccinate against tetanus, typhoid, and hepatitis A.

Bhutan has a varied topography, and the precautions you need to take will depend on where you are planning to go. If traveling to the subtropical, low-lying hills of southern Bhutan, where mosquitoes thrive, it is advisable to take antimalarial tablets and equip yourself with insect repellent.

Note that you will come across stray dogs in Bhutan—avoid them. If you are bitten by one, seek immediate medical help. It is advisable to be vaccinated against rabies.

It is important to become acclimatized before undertaking treks or strenuous activities, to avoid altitude sickness. If you should experience mild headaches or breathlessness and nausea, it is best to descend quickly. Tour guides are well trained to take appropriate action in such situations.

Sunburn in the high mountains can be vicious. A good sunscreen with an SPF of at least 30 is recommended. Also, slather on a generous quantity of insect repellent, and make sure to sleep under nets to avoid being bitten.

Health care is free in Bhutan, for visitors as well. Thimphu and other major towns have doctors and fairly well-equipped hospitals if the need arises. Smaller towns and remote villages have basic health units with trained health assistants to render medical help if needed. Comprehensive travel and medical insurance is essential. If you are taking any medication, take enough supplies and also a copy of the prescription with you. Generic medicines are available free of charge in the hospitals, and most can be bought at the pharmacies, with or without prescriptions. Tour guides are generally equipped with basic first-aid kits.

Avoid drinking untreated water or drinks with ice as most water resources in Bhutan are untreated (even though they have their source in the mountains). Bottled water is readily available, and most tour companies provide this free during the tours. It is best to boil or filter untreated water to prevent diarrhea, dysentery, and other infections.

Food can also transmit disease. Avoid salads, unpeeled fruit, reheated foods, and food that has been left out in the sun. Also avoid unpasteurized dairy products, as these can transmit a range of diseases.

NATURAL HAZARDS

Earthquakes

Bhutan is in an earthquake zone. The last tremor that caused minor structural damage to buildings was in 2009. Although no substantial disaster has taken place, experts believe that a major one is long overdue. In the wake of the 2015 earthquake disaster in neighboring Nepal, which left thousands dead, the government has set up a disaster-management department and put together a relief-response team. Earthquake drills are carried out in schools. Revised building regulations also ensure that buildings incorporate earthquake codes to ensure the safety of the structures.

Flash Floods and Landslides

Bhutan has twenty-five potentially dangerous glacial lakes created by melting glaciers. The most disastrous lake outburst was in 1994; it killed twenty people and destroyed homes, livestock, and farmland. Geologists believe that another lake—the Thorthormi—would pose imminent danger if it were to burst its banks, and would destroy everything in its path downstream. Efforts are in place to reduce this threat through the creation of various drainage channels.

Heavy monsoon rains between July and August swell small streams and rivers, washing away low-lying roads and bridges, and causing major landslides across the country, cutting off roads for days on end.

BANNED TOBACCO PRODUCTS

Since 2005 Bhutan has successfully banned the sale of tobacco and tobacco products, and it is important for visitors not to infringe these laws. Though the sale has been banned, consumption is not prohibited except in areas identified as smoke-free zones, such as public places, offices, and government premises. It is also sacrilegious to smoke near temples and any other religious sites. Cigarettes, pipe tobacco, and other tobacco products can be imported for personal use below a specific import quantity (e.g., 200 cigarettes, with payment of a 200 percent import duty and a valid receipt). Tobacco products cannot be imported for sale. Those in violation of the ban will be fined and serve a prison term. Shops and hotels caught selling them will lose their business licenses.

These laws were made to create a smoke-free nation with "no pollution and good health for the citizens." However, many observe that the ban has had little impact on curbing tobacco use and has instead given way to illegal trade.

CRIME

Bhutan is one of the safest countries in the world, and crime levels are remarkably low. The chance of being bitten by a stray dog is greater than that of being robbed on a street corner. However, it is always good to come prepared for any mishap. Ensure that valuable belongings such as passports, cameras, and wallets are properly secured during trekking, to avoid losing them. It is also not wise, while sightseeing, to leave these items within view in a locked vehicle.

Until a decade ago, traveling in the south of the country, especially after entering through Assam, in India, was forbidden because of the presence of Indian insurgents who had infiltrated from across the border and settled in the dense southern jungle. In 2005 the Bhutanese government undertook a major operation to flush these insurgents out, and since then the region has been relatively calm and the roads open to Bhutanese traffic—although caution is still advisable.

CHAPTER EIGHT

BUSINESS BRIEFING

THE BUSINESS ENVIRONMENT

In 2020 the World Bank Group, in its annual Doing Business report, ranked Bhutan eighty-ninth of 189 economies around the world, and second in South Asia after India. Bhutan's business environment has come a long way since 2010, when it was ranked 146. Over the last two decades the government has made changes business regulations, including enabling individuals to open and run small- and medium-sized businesses.

The Bhutanese economy relies largely on trade with India, and the bulk of its imports and exports pass through India. As a result the Indian rupee is legal tender in Bhutan. Four local banks, an Indian bank, and a number of insurance companies provide commercial services to local businesses.

Hydroelectricity and tourism are the main sectors of the economy, which, apart from the civil service and agriculture (58 percent of the workforce), employ most of the Bhutanese. Natural resource-based processing and other manufacturing companies operate in southern Bhutan, closer to India, where labor is cheap. Most businesses are taxed at 30 percent; however, certain priority sectors defined in the Economic Development Policy of 2017 are often exempt from specific taxes and/or provided with incentives for investment.

Since Bhutan opened up the economy to Foreign Direct Investment (FDI) in 2002, it has seen a number of investments, particularly in tourism, hospitality, food and agriculture, and information technology.

Bhutan is considered to be a good destination for FDI, as it is located close to huge markets in India and has a well-educated workforce. Unlike other countries in South Asia, there are minimal disruptions to doing business in Bhutan and a stable business environment. Foreigners can, however, find the pace of business frustratingly slow, a situation not helped by the huge bureaucracy.

BUSINESS HOURS

The usual working day is eight hours, including an hour's lunch break from 1:00 p.m. to 2:00 p.m. Most offices, including government offices, work from 9:00 a.m. until 5:00 p.m. In the winter months, between October and March when the days are short

and cold, the working day ends an hour early, at
4:00 p.m., to enable people to get home early.

These working hours also apply to the private sector.
Government offices are closed on Saturdays, while
other establishments such as schools, banks, and private
companies work half a day, and most shops in the high
street close early. Only pharmacists and a few grocery
stores remain open much longer.

STATUS AND HIERARCHY

Bhutan is a hierarchical society, and this is reflected in
everyday dealings, as discussed in Chapter 2. Highly
educated people with good family backgrounds
command respect and admiration. Self-made
individuals are admired but don't garner as much
respect as someone from a family of good standing.
However, this is changing, and most Bhutanese now
see the value of entrepreneurship. The Bhutanese accept
a hierarchical order in which everybody has a place.
Decisions are made top-down, and the boss ultimately
makes the final decision. Subordinates expect to be told
what to do, and they respect the boss's authority.

WOMEN AT WORK

As we have seen, women in Bhutan enjoy greater
equality than in most neighboring countries, and, with
modern development and access to education, more

and more are taking up work to contribute to the family income or to be financially independent individuals. Women make up around 37 percent of the civil service workforce, which is an improvement on the mere 16 percent of twenty years ago. However, only around 10 percent of these are in top executive positions, and only 15 percent of political positions are held by women. The picture in the private sector is different, with a significant number of women running successful private companies and an increasing number of female entrepreneurs making their mark in the business world.

Bhutanese women do not face any discrimination in terms of salary, and Western women will find no problem in doing business with Bhutanese men.

DRESS CODE

The Bhutanese wear their national dress to the office— the *gho* for men and the *kira* for women. The ceremonial scarves—men's *kabney* and women's *rachu*—are required at all times in all government and private offices bearing the national flag. Any additional scarves, coats, or the thermal underwear that most Bhutanese men wear under their *gho* (especially in winter) are strictly prohibited while visiting the *dzongs*. The formal dress should be paired with smart shoes (and knee-length socks for men). Flipflops or slippers of any kind are prohibited. One can walk barefoot if no shoes can be found.

Most expatriates enjoy wearing the Bhutanese national dress to work; otherwise, regular business suits are appropriate. For casual wear, the Bhutanese are not too particular about style and fashion. As long as your dress sense is not too extreme or risqué, you, as a visitor, can be comfortable in your own style.

If you are visiting the *dzongs* or monasteries as a tourist, your dress needs to be modest and fairly formal. Short-sleeved shirts, T-shirts, and Bermuda shorts are not allowed.

MEETINGS

Personal Connection

In a culture where "everyone knows everyone," relationships are developed through personal connections. Things move much faster if one is introduced through a mutual acquaintance, especially if you are a foreigner and need to get a firm foothold for a successful business venture.

Appointments can be made by e-mail or a telephone call to the business contact's secretary, although dropping in unannounced, especially when seeking to meet someone for the first time, is not totally uncommon; a meeting may be possible if the person in question is available. Such walk-in meetings are even more acceptable in rural areas. Most office workers can converse in English, and you will have no problem communicating.

At the Meeting

The Bhutanese are casual about punctuality, and good-naturedly refer to it as "Bhutan Stretchable Time," so don't be surprised if you are kept waiting. Meetings are cordial, with pleasantries exchanged, and on first meeting you may be greeted with a *khadar*—the white, silky scarf presented to a visitor.

The meeting begins with small talk to break the ice, followed by tea served in the official's or boss's office, which usually has a seating area. This allows them to get to know you better, and they will ask about your background, family, and interests. The Bhutanese are hospitable by nature, and business meetings are no exception. You will be treated with great respect, as they put emphasis on your comfort. They will indicate when they are ready to get down to business.

The Bhutanese usually greet with a slight bow, with both hands extended forward for a quick, closed handshake and a "*Kuzuzangpo-la*." While all meetings with foreigners are conducted in English, you will often hear the word "*la*" used at the end of a sentence as a mark of respect while addressing another person. For instance, "Do you agree, *la*?" If conducting meetings with representatives of rural communities, you will have an interpreter to translate for you.

It is important to note that the Bhutanese don't make direct eye contact with the person they are talking to. And if the person is considered to be high ranking, they will maintain respectful body language, with a slight bow of the head. They don't use busy hand movements to express their thoughts, and they will listen to you intently with little interruption. As we have seen, it is considered impolite to say "no" directly; the Bhutanese tend to avoid direct confrontation and look for an alternative way to convey disagreement.

Meetings are concluded with an exchange of business cards and often with a parting gift. It is considered polite to walk the guest to the door, where a final round of greetings and good-byes are said.

PRESENTATIONS

There are no hard-and-fast rules when it comes to making a presentation. The skills desired elsewhere are applicable in Bhutan, too. Presentations should be clear, comprehensible, and visually attractive, but not distractingly elaborate. It is important that attention be paid to content, with correct and well-researched facts and figures and enough graphics and images for visual appeal. Try to keep things short, and leave plenty of time for discussion at the end. The Bhutanese will focus more on your abilities, your experience, and what you can offer rather than on your presentation skills. Impact is often created up front rather than during the presentation.

The Bhutanese don't usually ask questions, not wishing to cause the presenter any offense or embarrassment. They prefer to give feedback after the session, in a smaller group or private meeting.

Decisions are consensus driven, and often require the engagement of the stakeholders, even after a specific meeting. Some individuals prefer to go back to their office and discuss matters with their colleagues and superiors. It is useful to follow up with an e-mail and meeting notes, to ensure that promised actions are completed.

NEGOTIATING

When it comes to negotiations, remember that the Bhutanese are not hard bargainers and don't expect their counterparts to be so either. This may be attributable to the culture of humility and respect, which plays an important part in shaping people's attitudes. They prefer to solve disagreements in an amicable manner and avoid confrontations, with the final aim of arriving at a decision with mutual benefits.

However, the reluctance to drive a hard bargain can delay or slow down the whole negotiation process, and it may take several meetings to arrive at an agreement. In addition, there is the complex culture of politeness and honor involved, which means the Bhutanese are not always forthright with their opinions, looking for ways to avoid saying "no" to save face—both their own and their counterpart's. It's important to be clear about what you want from them, but try not to criticize, to be too blunt, or to appear patronizing. Always leave room for some compromise. It's about give and take in equal measure.

CONTRACTS

It's important to employ a local lawyer (*jabmi*) to work on contractual issues. Once agreement is reached, a detailed contract is drawn up, which will cover all aspects of the business. These are generally written in English, but may be in Dzongkha as well, if required. Bhutanese contracts are governed by the provisions of the Evidence Act of 2005. All contracts, termed "written agreements," are signed by all parties in the presence of one witness each, and executed with a legal stamp. Given the superstitious nature of the Bhutanese, an astrologer may be consulted to determine the most favorable day and time for the contract to be signed.

The contract is rendered invalid if any word is erased or has a defective seal or signature. However, the contract is not all binding; it may be changed by agreement. Oral agreement is given much importance too. As work progresses, details in the contract may be modified with the agreement of both parties.

If there is some kind of dispute or disagreement between parties, the Bhutanese prefer to solve the matter amicably rather than take the disagreement to court.

BUSINESS ENTERTAINMENT

Socializing with your business partners is important. Breakfast meetings are not typical, but you will be invited for lunch or dinner in a popular restaurant in town. Business meals are long and informal, with a lot of food, drink, and laughter. This eases the atmosphere and provides an opportunity for both parties to get better acquainted and build up the relationship. These meals are often purely for entertainment, devoid of any business talk. For important delegation groups, there will be a lively cultural program arranged, with traditional singers and dancers, and as the evening progresses you may be invited to join in the dance. If you enjoy sports, you may be invited for a game of archery, Bhutan's much-loved national pastime.

If you are hosting a meal, make sure that there is plenty of food to go around. The Bhutanese think it is important to do things in abundance, and generous hospitality will demonstrate your good heart and welcoming nature.

GIFTS

In Bhutan, one never visits empty handed. Whether in the workplace or at home, the Bhutanese are particular when it comes to offering gifts, be it a small one (such as a bundle of *doma paani*) or something more significant. The gesture is regarded as thoughtful and appreciative. In a more formal setting, a gift is offered to a visitor at the end of a meeting, which indicates the beginning of a new relationship and the building of a good connection.

It is also interesting to note that in Bhutan an exchange of gifts depends on your social status. If one receives a present from someone of the same social status or ranking as oneself, one is expected to give a present in return. For example, if the guest brings food, the container is returned filled with sweets, cookies, or fruits—anything but empty. However, if the gift is from a high-ranking official or an individual of higher status than oneself, it is inappropriate to reciprocate with a gift. And unlike in the West, where a gift is opened in front of the presenter and appreciated, the Bhutanese do not open one in the presence of the giver. So don't be surprised if your gift is put away and nothing is mentioned about it later.

However, particularly in dealing with civil servants, you should be aware of the fact that expensive gifts may need to be declared to ensure that there is no conflict of interest. Therefore it is recommended that your gift be modest and not too expensive for a Bhutanese.

KEEPING IN TOUCH

Regular e-mail correspondence and phone calls are important for staying in touch, but don't expect prompt replies, especially to e-mails. When possible, regular visits in person are much more valued and appreciated, as this shows your genuine interest in building a long-term business relationship.

CHAPTER NINE

COMMUNICATING

LANGUAGE

Bhutan is a multilingual society with more than nineteen different languages, of which sixteen are purely oral. Given that the written script was mainly Buddhist scriptures and only monks could read and write, spoken languages retain a significant importance as the transmission media of folk stories and repositories of cultural knowledge and values, passed down over centuries.

Dzongkha, which is predominantly spoken in the west by the Ngalong, was made the official national language of Bhutan in 1960. It is closely related to Tibetan, but distinct in its style and character. It is written in the classical Tibetan script, the language of the religion. Dzongkha is taught in schools and spoken throughout the country. It is also used in official communications, and a government department exists to develop and promote the use of the language. The vernacular version is easier than the one used officially.

Tshangla, or Sharchopka, spoken in the east, is entirely different from Dzongkha, as is Nepali, spoken in the southern regions of Bhutan among the Lhotshampa communities. In addition there are common languages and dialects, such as Khyengkha, Kurtopkha, and Bumthangkha, and lesser-known languages, such as Chocha Ngacha, Drokha, and Dakpakha in Merak and Sakteng. The development of these separate languages is a consequence of the country's mountainous topography, in which people lived in different remote or almost inaccessible valleys, with little or no interaction. The variety of languages has woven a rich tapestry and brought about diverse traditions in the valleys, and the oral stories have formed a significant store of historical knowledge.

Today both English and Dzongkha are used for teaching in schools and institutions. This makes it easier for foreigners to communicate with the Bhutanese. English is often seen as a very good tool for the preservation of the Bhutanese cultural heritage, from documenting Bhutanese folklore to codifying cultural practices, lest they be lost.

As we have seen, the use of "*la*" after any sentence or phrase is a gesture to indicate politeness and respect. It is widely used, even when speaking English, with expressions such as "How are you, *la*?" or "Yes, *la*."

Languages Spoken at Home

Thus, for a small society, Bhutan has a rich and interesting collection of languages and dialects, spoken across different valleys and regions. Except for the national language, Dzongkha, the regional and tribal languages have no written form. Given the increasing integration of people from across Bhutan, enabled by communications, roads, and intermarriages, it is not uncommon to find different members of the family conversing in different languages. The children may speak in their own regional language to their parents, but use Dzongkha or English—two common languages spoken by the young population—when speaking to each other. Hindi, from Indian TV, seems to have a great influence on young children, who often ask their parents to speak in Hindi while speaking to them.

BODY LANGUAGE

The Bhutanese are generally reserved and physically controlled. The cultural emphasis on being polite and respectful is reflected in their body language. While interacting with superiors, or with someone you have just met, it is considered correct to stand with a slightly bent back and not make direct eye contact. The attitude of "shoulders back, chin up, and head held high" that is acceptable in the West would not be approved of in Bhutan, where it would be regarded as self-important. The Bhutanese usually extend both hands for a handshake, with a little nod of the head, when meeting someone for the first time.

It is important to remember to sit cross-legged when sitting on the floor. It is bad manners to stretch out your legs in front of you. If you cannot sit cross-legged, it is

better to tell your host and opt for a chair or the bed to sit on. It is considered rude to cross your legs with the feet pointing at the other person, or to point a finger when referring to or showing something.

Animated hand gestures are not encouraged, unless you are in an informal setting, relaxing with family and friends. Instead they indicate something with an open palm, with all fingers pointing in the direction of reference.

HUMOR

The Bhutanese are very ready to laugh, and there are some popular comedians who are well known for their slapstick comedy, impressions, and caricatures. Bhutanese humor generally tends to be slapstick, and it is also colorful and bawdy. It is often laced with double-entendres in the tradition of Lama Drukpa

Kuenley, the "Divine Madman," and like the playful and mischievous *atsaras* (festival clowns), who swing wooden phalluses and make lewd jokes for the amusement of the crowd.

Word play and wit are part and parcel of archery games, where women cheerleaders from the opposing team sing insulting jokes to distract the archers.

Stereotypical jokes are common, and people often make casual generalizations and jokes about those from other regions. The Tshentops from Paro are regarded as hotheaded and ready with their fists if provoked, and

Pemagatshelpas (from Pemagatshel in the east) are mocked for their short stature. But none are subjected to more ridicule than the Uzurongpas (from the village of Uzurong in Trashigang). They are often portrayed as dim-witted and are the butt of many jokes.

The Bhutanese will happily joke about most things, including themselves, but any humor or jokes directed at the royals, the clergy, or the authorities are not appreciated, and should be strictly avoided.

THE MEDIA

The Bhutanese media is fairly young. It began in 1965 with the establishment of *Kuensel*, then a government-funded weekly newspaper that mainly published government development activities and programs. *Kuensel* was privatized in 1992 and now prints daily. Soon, radio—the Bhutan Broadcasting Service (BBS)—came into being in 1973. For a long time, *Kuensel* and BBS radio were the only two news outlets. This changed in 1999, when, as a special celebration on the twenty-fifth anniversary of the coronation of the fourth king, the virtual world of television and the Internet were finally introduced into Bhutan.

The progress in the last few decades has been tremendous. Today, there are nine newspapers (a few folded after a short stint), magazines, a few private FM radio stations like Radio Valley (only in Thimphu) and Kuzoo FM, and numerous satellite channels from across the world through cable TV. BBS radio broadcasts nationwide and is still the only communication medium for the remote villages. BBS TV is widely watched for the local news (broadcast both in Dzongkha and English) and local programs. Besides numerous soap operas, Bhutan also has *Druk Superstar*, its own version of *American Idol* for local singing sensations, which is very popular with the viewers.

TV and radio are more popular than print in the country, where the illiteracy rate is still high at 37 percent. Indian channels, with their numerous soap operas, are loved and watched by the majority of Bhutanese, and there is no censorship in general. Indian films, made in Hindi, have always been popular with film lovers.

Early on, many raised concerns about the negative impact of outside influence on Bhutanese society. Articles reported that children were wrestling violently, like the World Wrestling Entertainment fighters they saw on TV, and parents worried about their young children wanting to speak only foreign languages. Many, however, argue that the Bhutanese have a strong sense of their own culture and identity, and that the exposure and knowledge acquired only enhance and broaden their horizons.

MAIL

Bhutan's mail service began in 1962. In those days the service was slow and sporadic, taking weeks for mail—often carried on horseback and sometimes on foot—to be delivered across the country. Bhutan Post now has around eighty-nine outlets throughout the country, and also provides fast and reliable international shipping such as Express Mail Service (EMS), FedEx, and money-order services, among others. The main Post Office in Thimphu is in the heart of the town, in Chang Lam, next to the Bhutan National Bank.

While the international postal service is impressive, with letters sent to an address in the West often arriving within a week, the domestic postal service still leaves much to be desired. Letters take weeks to arrive, and letters or parcels are sometimes misdirected or lost. It is best to send important letters and parcels by registered post to ensure their safe delivery. Thimphu now has international courier services such as DHL, which, although more expensive, offers swift and efficient deliveries to anywhere in the world.

Memorable Stamps
What it lacks in service Bhutan makes up for in its interesting philatelic history. Since the introduction of the mail service Bhutan has produced exotic collections of stamps, ranging from studies of local flora and fauna to colorful depictions of Buddhist mask dances. The most prized stamps among collectors are the "talking stamps"—actual miniature vinyl records with recordings of the Bhutanese national anthem, folksongs, and a historical narrative in Dzongkha and English. It was an American entrepreneur, Burt Todd, also the first American to set foot in the country, who helped to create these stamps.

TELEPHONE

As with the rest of the world, landline telephone usage is declining in Bhutan as more Bhutanese opt for cell phones. Currently Bhutan Telecom Ltd. and Tashi Info-Comm. Ltd. provide cell-phone services with fairly good coverage in the bigger towns, such as Thimphu and Paro. However, if you are traveling, the connection outside the towns will be poor.

If you want to make international calls, while it may be convenient to use your own phone with international roaming capabilities, it would be cheaper to get a local SIM card and prepaid or rechargeable vouchers. You will need to have your phone unlocked to use the local SIM card. You can buy one for Nu. 100 from any mobile shop upon providing a photocopy of your passport. Many hotels can also arrange local and international calls for a premium, or you could visit one of the telecommunications shops in the market to call abroad and send faxes. Local calls cost around Nu. 1 per minute, and international calls to the USA or to the UK cost around Nu. 18 per minute.

INTERNET AND SOCIAL MEDIA

As with cell phones, Internet usage is fast picking up. Both fixed (wired) and mobile broadband are available, and Druknet (part of Bhutan Telecom) and Drukcom are the two ISPs providing fixed (wired) broadband Internet services in the country.

There are a few Internet cafés in the major towns, where the connection is fairly good. Many of the hotels also offer free Wi-Fi in their lobby areas, but the connections are poor in the smaller towns, and may not be as reliable or as fast as you are used to.

Platforms including Facebook and Twitter are popular among many Bhutanese, while Instagram, Snapchat, and TikTok are particularly popular with younger people. Messaging services such as WhatsApp and WeChat are also widely used. As in many countries, the rapid adoption of social media has meant a steep learning curve for many when it comes to important issues such as the proliferation of unverified news stories.

CONCLUSION

It was in the early 1960s, when America was working toward landing on the moon, that Bhutan built its first road and the first motorized transportation made its maiden journey across the mountains, launching this previously secluded country into modern times. That was more than fifty years ago, and since then Bhutan has seen unprecedented progress and prosperity—all on its own terms. Its Gross National Happiness policy provides an example of how to prioritize the wellbeing and happiness of a people by embracing the preservation of the natural environment, cultural identity, and local traditions as part of its development agenda.

This proud, shrewd, and resilient people, with their open attitude, giving nature, and unique cultural heritage, make an indelible impression on all who meet them. Your visit will leave you with no doubt that Bhutan is truly the last Shangri-la—no longer hidden within the folds of the mighty Himalayas.

FURTHER READING

Choden, Kunzang. *Folktales of Bhutan*. Bangkok, Thailand: White Lotus, 1994.

Das, Britta. *Buttertea at Sunrise: A Year in the Bhutan Himalaya*. Chichester, UK: Summersdale Publishers Limited, 2006.

Hickman, Katie. *Dreams of the Peaceful Dragon: A Journey through Bhutan*. Phoenix, USA: Phoenix Publishing, 2002.

Leaming, Linda. *A Field Guide to Happiness: What I Learned in Bhutan about Living, Loving, and Waking Up*. Carlsbad: Hay House Inc, 2014.

Phuntsho, Karma. *The History of Bhutan*. New York: Vintage, 2016.

Ura, Karma. *The Hero with a Thousand Eyes: A Historical Novel*. Thimphu, Bhutan: Karma Ura, 1995.

Wangchuck, Ashi Dorji Wangmo, Queen of Bhutan. *Treasures of the Thunder Dragon: A Portrait of Bhutan*. India: Viking, 2006.

Zeppa, Jamie. *Beyond the Sky and the Earth: A journey into Bhutan*. Toronto, Canada: Doubleday Canada, 2000.

Useful Web Sites
www.mohca.gov.bt (Ministry of Home and Culture)
www.mfa.gov.bt (Foreign Ministry)
www.health.gov.bt (Health Ministry)
www.bhutanstudies.org.bt (Centre for Bhutan Studies, think tank)
www.tourism.gov.bt (Tourism Council of Bhutan)

Media Web Sites
www.kuenselonline.com Kuensel (daily newspaper)
www.bbs.bt (Bhutan Broadcasting Services, TV/radio)
www.businessbhutan.bt (Business Bhutan, weekly English newspaper)
www.thebhutanese.bt (The Bhutanese, weekly English newspaper)

Other Web Sites
www.drukair.com.bt (Druk Air, national airline)
www.bcci.org.bt (Bhutan Chamber of Commerce and Industry)
www.ncwc.gov.bt (National Commission for Women and Children, autonomous agency)
www.rspnbhutan.org (Royal Society for Protection of Nature, non-profit environment organization)
www.loden.org (Loden Foundation, supports entrepreneurship)

USEFUL APPS

Though local app makers are still finding their feet and are not yet as advanced as those in neighboring China or India, there are already a few promising local services. These will likely continue to improve over time as their usage and popularity grow. Here is a list of the most useful apps that were functional at the time of publication:

Transport: **DrukRide** – this local ride-hailing app is most functional in and around Thimphu. Helpfully, the app also sells bus tickets and provides travel information. Another option is **Oie Drive**.

Food: **DrukFood** and **Dish8Door** are online food delivery services.

Banking: **mBoB** – Bank of Bhutan's app allows account holders to transfer money, pay utility bills and make payments in shops and restaurants. **BNB mPAY** – A similar banking app to mBoB, but for Bhutan National Bank account holders.

PICTURE CREDITS

INDEX